Praise for *Saying Is Believing*

"*Saying Is Believing* establishes Amanda Drury as a new and compelling voice in practical theology, a pacesetter for a generation of scholars convinced that the way we form young people's faith profoundly affects our own. Drury quickly nuances and moves beyond the commonly cited research on teenagers' religious inarticulacy; a natural storyteller, she makes theologically rich analysis easy to digest, and serves it alongside generous portions of practical wisdom for helping young people learn to speak their convictions. *Saying Is Believing* is less about problems than solutions, which makes it a must-have resource for anyone who takes young people's faith seriously."

Kenda Creasy Dean, Princeton Theological Seminary, author of *Almost Christian: What the Faith of Our Teenagers Is Telling the American Church*

"Amanda Drury is one of the most creative and thoughtful people thinking about youth ministry in North America. Mandy has the rare talent to seamlessly blend deep theological ideas with TV shows, parenting and her own experiences in youth ministry. She writes and speaks effortlessly, with numerous creative turns along the way. As Mandy presents in this book, testimony has become a lost element in the church, and its loss has been at the detriment of our youth, as they've been neglected the nourishment that is dependent on testimony for active Christian living. The stories of God's action in each of our lives are the meal that gives our young people the strength and vision to seek God. *Saying Is Believing* addresses the famine of testimony we face and promises a feast for the reader and the ministry he or she is called to lead."

Andrew Root, Luther Seminary, author of *The Relational Pastor and Bonhoeffer as Youth Worker*

"When it comes to helping young people develop their own spiritual identities, few things are as important as helping them discover an authentic vocabulary for their faith. With our focus on missions and programs, helping youth articulate their faith often gets lost in the shuffle. But Amanda Drury teaches us how—and brilliantly. It won't take more than a few chapters to reveal that Mandy is one of the most profound, accessible, original voices ever to speak into the conversation about youth ministry."

Mark DeVries, author of *Sustainable Youth Ministry*

"I love it when I discover an area in my youth ministry practice or thinking where I was wrong. This is God's ongoing revelation to me, peeling back misconceptions and malpractices, causing growth in my life and practice of youth ministry. Amanda Drury's book winsomely confronted me and conclusively helped me rediscover a critically important aspect of adolescent spiritual formation that I—along with thousands of my youth ministry peers—had gradually relegated to the youth ministry storage closet in the basement of the church. Time for a course correction, time for growth, time for testimony."

Mark Oestreicher, partner, The Youth Cartel, author of *Hopecasting: Finding, Keeping and Sharing the Things Unseen*

"Thoughtful, practical and creative, Drury's book opens up new perspectives on ministry with young people. One of the most original and helpful contributions to practical theology in recent years."

Richard Osmer, Princeton Theological Seminary

"Amanda Drury has done youth ministry—and the church as a whole—a great service by recovering the lost practice of testimony. If we truly desire to see youth develop a winsome, robust and enduring faith identity, we cannot afford to neglect her call. Both thought-provoking and inspiring, Drury's *Saying Is Believing* represents practical theology at its best."

David Setran, Wheaton College

Saying Is Believing

The Necessity of Testimony in Adolescent Spiritual Development

AMANDA HONTZ DRURY

IVP Academic

An imprint of InterVarsity Press
Downers Grove, Illinois

InterVarsity Press
P.O. Box 1400, Downers Grove, IL 60515-1426
ivpress.com
email@ivpress.com

InterVarsity Press® is the book-publishing division of InterVarsity Christian Fellowship/USA®, a movement of students and faculty active on campus at hundreds of universities, colleges and schools of nursing in the United States of America, and a member movement of the International Fellowship of Evangelical Students. For information about local and regional activities, visit intervarsity.org.

All Scripture quotations, unless otherwise indicated, are taken from THE HOLY BIBLE, NEW INTERNATIONAL VERSION®, NIV® Copyright © 1973, 1978, 1984, 2011 by Biblica, Inc.™ Used by permission. All rights reserved worldwide.

While any stories in this book are true, some names and identifying information may have been changed to protect the privacy of individuals.

Cover design: Cindy Kiple
Interior design: Beth McGill
Image: desifoto/Getty Images

ISBN 978-0-8308-4065-6 (print)
ISBN 978-0-8308-9701-8 (digital)

Printed in the United States of America ♾

g **green**
press
INITIATIVE *As a member of the Green Press Initiative, InterVarsity Press is committed to protecting the environment and to the responsible use of natural resources. To learn more, visit greenpressinitiative.org.*

Library of Congress Cataloging-in-Publication Data

A catalog record for this book is available from the Library of Congress.

P	23	22	21	20	19	18	17	16	15	14	13	12	11	10	9	8	7	6	5	4	3	2	1
Y	35	34	33	32	31	30	29	28	27	26	25	24	23	22	21	20	19	18	17	16	15		

This book is dedicated to my parents,

Paul and Marilyn Hontz,

who modeled for me at an early age

what it meant to live in

"perpetual advent."

Contents

Acknowledgments

Thanks to those of you who have participated in various interviews and surveys: Jeff Brady, Charlie Alcock, David Kujawa, Jason Brewer, Chopper Brown, Keith Drury, Madison Swink, Kayla Gunsalus and the many other teenagers who graciously told me their stories.

This book would not have been possible without my doctoral adviser, Richard Osmer, who always seemed to know exactly where to direct me regarding my research. Thanks as well to my mentor, Kenda Dean, who ushered me into the world of youth ministry in the first place. I am grateful.

Thanks to my children, Sam, Clara and Paul, who have supported me in writing this book in their own ways.

Thank you to my husband and best friend, John, for sending me on writing retreats, bringing me coffee and offering both suggestions and encouragement along the way.

1

Testimony

An Introduction

*As [Jesus] was getting into the boat, the man who had been possessed
by demons begged him that he might be with him. But Jesus refused,
and said to him, "Go home to your friends, and tell them how much
the Lord has done for you, and what mercy he has shown you." And
he went away and began to proclaim in the Decapolis how much
Jesus had done for him; and everyone was amazed.*

MARK 5:18-20

As a child, I always entered the sanctuary hoping to see microphones in the aisles. A microphone in the aisle meant that we would be hearing from more than the pastor during that service. A microphone in the aisle meant there would be space in the service for an individual to stand up and share carte blanche what was on her heart. While you never knew what might happen, there was a certain level of predictability. If Mrs. Goodman was present, there would be tears along with references to a difficult childhood. If Mr. Copper was present, we would hear a quasi-prophetic rant with a call to a deeper life of holiness. I remember ragged breathing into a corded, portable microphone with a large ball-like muffler as the speaker summoned the courage to tackle the monster of public speaking. Every once in a while a child my age would stand and make a rapid-fire statement publicly praising a godly mother, often prompting sentimental feelings from the listeners. While I heard stories of freedom from addictions in the past, I don't recall any dramatic confessions of present entanglements in sordid circumstances; of course, one could always hope.

Testimonies were exhilarating to my child's mind. You never knew what was going to happen. Anyone could stand up and say anything. If we were lucky we would get a fresh story about someone from the church that had a torrid past from which he or she had found freedom. Drugs, alcohol, some had even been in jail. Of course, these testimonies were not the norm. Most testimonies consisted of small blessings people had seen that week. Others were more akin to prayer requests with a confession of belief tagged on at the end. So a woman might stand up and speak of her wayward child and end with something along the lines of, "But I know that God will be faithful and I'm trusting he will intervene." Then there were those testimonies that were simple pronouncements of thankfulness: "I just want to thank the Lord," some would say, "for . . ." and then they would fill in the blank with wherever they sensed the presence of God the week before.

A microphone in the aisle was a symbol of excitement for my eight-year-old mind. A microphone in the aisle was a symbol of terror for my father, who was pastor. A microphone in the aisle meant one thing: it was time to testify.

My exhilaration was also due in part to fear. Not knowing who was going to speak nor what was going to be said, I always had a small fear that someone was going to stand up and publicly critique my father, the head pastor. This never happened to my recollection (though he might say otherwise), but even at a young age I was very aware of the possibility of someone hijacking a service.

I recently asked my father about the anxiety surrounding the unknown testimonies. He could not help but laugh and explain, "It's kinda like that old Forrest Gump line where he's sitting at the bus bench and he says to the lady, 'Life is like a box of chocolates, you never know what you're going to get.'"[1] He elucidates: "Whenever we've held open-mic

---

[1] Paul Hontz, interview by Amanda Drury, digital recording, Central Wesleyan Church, Holland, Michigan, December 19, 2011.

testimonies for whoever wished to share, it was oftentimes a hold-your-breath experience because some people saw it as an opportunity to tell a story that probably edified no one but themselves."[2]

I remember a childhood conversation with my father about a particular congregant who had a tendency to testify at every opportunity. "Why does she always cry?" I asked my dad. I do not remember his exact answer, but I do remember picking up on some annoyance in his voice. Looking back I have little doubt this annoyance was probably properly directed toward what was most likely an emotionally charged, tangential testimony with little edification taking place.

Also exciting were the believers' baptismal testimonies given just prior to immersion. These testimonies produced less anxiety for me as a listener because I knew they were written out ahead of time and gone over with a pastor on staff. I still have my own baptismal testimony written out in pencil on the front and back of a three-by-five card from when I was ten years old. Again, I was drawn toward the dramatic, sensational stories where grown men with shaking hands and voice would describe their lives before surrendering to the Lord. Many spoke of former addictions or of lives steeped in anger. Many also spoke of being raised by godly parents but deciding to run away from God in their teenage years. I remember hearing these prodigal son stories and thinking, *I'm still going to love God when I'm a teenager, no matter what.* At a very young age I was given a road map of potential pitfalls in the Christian life: avoid drugs and alcohol, and do not get pulled away by "the wrong crowd." Of course, there were those peers of mine who heard these same testimonies and assumed it meant they could live wild lives as teenagers and still have the opportunity to "come back to the Lord" after they became adults.

Space for testimonies was also given following a missions trip or a youth camp. Often the church had offered financial support for these endeavors, and testifying was a way in which the congregants could hear how their giving helped fund some ministry outside of our own four walls.

It was sometime in the late 1980s or early 1990s that our church began to move from spontaneous testimonies to those that were more ordered

---

[2]Ibid.

and planned. The microphones in the aisles were saved primarily for church business meetings in case a congregant had a question about the budget. The church was experiencing significant growth which made overseeing spontaneous testimonies more and more difficult.

Baptismal testimonies underwent their own transition. We moved from live testimonies to videotaped and edited testimonies that were shown on large screens. The church explored alternate creative ways to share testimonies—particularly when baptisms were moved to Lake Michigan or to the church's large outdoor pond where sound amplification was an issue. Sunday mornings would occasionally have those being baptized walk across the stage holding up large signs. One side of the sign described life without Christ, the other side described life with Christ. So a man might walk across with a poster that read "Addicted" on one side and "Freed" on the other. Another woman might have "Bitter" written on one side of her poster and "Peaceful" on the other. I remember this being a very moving scene to witness. These people were later celebrated with a picnic dinner prior to being baptized outside. Those wanting to hear more of their testimonies could pick up a small booklet to read their testimonies at length.

The church still practices testifying apart from what takes place at baptisms, but even these testimonies are quite different than what I remember from my childhood. Many of these testimonies are given on Sunday mornings—either via video or in what might be described as "testimonial interviews" where a member of the pastoral staff will pre-arrange for a congregant to join him or her on stage to answer a few questions about where and how God has been at work in his or her life.

> **It was not until much later in my life that I realized the stories I heard as an eight-year-old were more than descriptive narratives of the speaker's past; these stories were actually forming our present and future selves.**

These early, formative experiences at my church planted a seed, which grew into a hunch and eventually developed into the heart of this book: the role and function of testimony plays an integral part in the spiritual formation of adolescents. It was not until much later in my life that I realized the stories I heard as an eight-year-old were more than descriptive narratives of the speaker's past; those stories were actually forming our present and future selves. *Those who testified were doing more than describing; they were constructing.*

In the past, I understood testifying in the most rudimentary terms: a testimony was a story someone told about her experience with God. Testimonies, in my mind, were largely descriptive narratives of something that occurred in the past. What I didn't realize, however, was that the testimonies shared went beyond mere description and moved into the realm of construction. People were not just describing the past; people were being changed as they spoke. And this kind of construction was not just present for the speaker; those of us receiving the testimony were also being formed.

The following chapters draw from various narrative theories of the social sciences to support this claim. When an individual is able to articulate where and how he understands God to be present in his life, this articulation can serve as a kind of legitimating apparatus, and one's description of God's presence in the past may help bolster one's present faith. Again, this kind of buttressing can be present not only for the speaker but also for those on the receiving end of the testimony.

The emergence of adolescence is an ideal time for this kind of articulation to be cultivated. It is in these early adolescent years that most individuals begin to understand their lives in storied, historic terms. As clinical psychologist Daniel McAdams states, there is a "development of formal thought and the emergence of a historical perspective of the self."[3]

This pairing of the adolescent construction of the self with articulacy theories surrounding the practice of testifying is of particular interest to me especially in light of the various reports concerning teenagers, articulacy and faith retention as presented by Christian Smith and Melinda Denton in the National Study on Youth and Religion as well as the findings behind the "sticky faith" research out of Fuller Seminary. This articulacy theory of testimony is a timely and important concept to highlight particularly as these national studies are revealing staggering reports of religious inarticulacy among adolescents growing up within the church.

Painting in broad strokes, one could say testifying tends to be more prevalent in particular ecclesial circles. I was not surprised to find strands

---

[3]Daniel P. McAdams, *The Stories We Live By: Personal Myths and the Making of the Self* (New York: W. Morrow, 1993), p. 12.

of this practice in my Wesleyan Methodist tradition, nor in various Pentecostal or certain African American churches. You could say that testifying runs in my ecclesial blood—or at least, it *did*. There is anecdotal evidence of the practice of testifying diminishing as local churches found themselves in more respectable, professional settings. As clergy became more professionalized, the practice of testifying seemed to dwindle. Why put a microphone in front of a layperson when we have a highly educated pastor to speak on our behalf?

My home church is somewhat of an anomaly in that they still testify in one form or another. Many churches that have historically practiced testifying now shy away from this practice, throwing the proverbial baby out with the bathwater as ministerial positions become more professionalized. Given that, it was curious for me to observe the decline of testifying in more evangelical settings and the testimony's subsequent emergence in more mainline settings. Reverend Lillian Daniel of First Congregational Church in Glen Ellyn, Illinois, is a prime example of the latter. Her experience at Church of the Redeemer in New Haven, Connecticut, shared in her book *Tell It Like It Is*, paints a clear picture of what the practice of testimony looks like in a more mainline setting, as does Thomas Long's *Testimony: Talking Ourselves into Being Christian*.[4]

Regardless of the ebb and flow of testifying, what is clear is that this practice is in no way limited to a particular branch of Christian faith, nor is it limited to a particular age. In fact, in my own tradition, while the role of testifying has diminished in the overall life of the church, there have been pockets of testimonial resurgence among some teenagers. One of these pockets is at City Life Church in Grand Rapids, Michigan, a church that provides space for young and old to testify. Jovhana is one of those teenagers with a story to share.

JOVHANA'S TESTIMONY

It was the second Sunday of Advent. Jovhana stood with the congregation of City Life Church as they sang carols. She listened to announcements

---

[4]Lillian Daniel, *Tell It Like It Is: Reclaiming the Practice of Testimony* (Herndon, VA: Alban Institute, 2006); and Thomas Long, *Testimony: Talking Ourselves into Being Christian* (San Francisco: Jossey-Bass, 2004).

concerning the Christmas cards for local prisoners. She made mental notes of the times of the upcoming Christmas services. She listened to the children's choir sing their slightly off rendition of "Gentle Mary, Humble Mary." Offering was taken, a sermon preached, and then it was Jovhana's turn.

Her youth pastor introduced her as she walked on stage and picked up the microphone, "Early in my life I was passed around from my mother to my father," she began.[5] "I really didn't have a stable home, and suddenly I was in foster care because my mom was said to be an 'unfit parent.' I was only one year old. I stayed in foster care for two years. I don't remember much, but eventually I was adopted."[6] The congregation was silent, captivated with her story.

Jovhana went on to explain the emotional struggles that went along with these rocky transitions: "I felt as though I had no one. . . . I was hurting. I guess I didn't feel God's presence. I was angry, scared and completely insecure."

And then, in front of sixty people, Jovhana described a youth group experience where she first became cognizant of God's love. This realization, she claims, was life-changing: "I was filled with love! And all my feelings of hatred toward myself were somehow forgotten in that moment."[7]

Jovhana was about to be baptized, and she wanted her church family to hear the story that brought her to the water. City Life was a six-year-old church plant in the middle of inner-city Grand Rapids. The 130 congregants who attended both services could not be more diverse. Mixed within the suburban families were prostitutes and addicts. The church was strategically planted near the largest mission of the area, which meant City Life had a large population of congregants who could name their home *church* but not a home *address*. This was Jovhana's church. And although her earthly family was not there to witness her baptism, she had found another family within the church's four walls. And so on the second Sunday of Advent, speaking to her church family in her gray T-shirt and black sweatpants, preparing to be immersed into the horse

---

[5]Jovhana, interview by Amanda Drury, written record, City Life Church morning worship service, Grand Rapids, Michigan, December 4, 2011.
[6]Ibid.
[7]Ibid.

trough that served the young congregation as a baptismal font, Jovhana told her story.

She announced she wanted to be baptized because she wanted "God to recognize me making that huge step." She saw it as her way of saying, "Okay, here I am Lord! Have your way with me."[8] Jovhana claims she was extremely nervous as she walked to the stage. Her nerves melted away, however, the more she spoke. Her voice strengthened as she came to her conclusion:

> I know this is just the beginning. I'm ready to go on this journey with Jesus! I know I am not perfect but I'm willing to be anything God wants me to be. . . . I want to go on mission trips and help as many of God's people as I can. That's the last thing he asked of us before he left this earth. I plan on letting the Spirit guide me and take me where I need to be. Jesus means everything to me. . . . The thought that Jesus loved each and every one of us so much that he gave his life just for us . . . that alone is astonishing; it never ceases to amaze me that this could be true. Jesus is awesome![9]

Figure 1.1. Jovhana's baptism. Photo by Christy Lipscomb. Used with permission.

Jovhana was the first convert of the church's small youth group. And to cheers and applause of friends and strangers alike, Jovhana, once a neglected child, symbolically buried her old life and began her life anew. Jovhana did more than undergo the rite of baptism on that Advent Sunday. Jovhana testified.

This act of testifying is unusual for several reasons. First, public speaking is often identified as a fearful experience. Why would a teenager *choose* to speak in public? Second, teenagers are not known for being articulate on spiritual matters. And finally, as mentioned earlier, many churches are shying away from this practice of public testimony

---

[8]Ibid.
[9]Ibid.

for numerous reasons. Despite these barriers, on this particular Sunday evening, Jovhana testified. And she would tell you, along with the sixty other people sitting in the sanctuary, that she is different because of it. Jovhana would be among the first to confirm the thesis that *engaging in the practice of testimony develops and deepens authentic Christian faith for adolescents.*

DEFINING TESTIMONY

Often when people hear the word *testimony*, their minds are drawn to one of two images. The first is a courtroom, complete with stand and jury box, where an individual is called on to offer either eyewitness or expert testimony. There is good reason why this image comes to mind. We have centuries and centuries of examples of various court systems where testimonies are given. Wherever there has been a quest for truth, testimonies have closely followed. In our legal systems today we often speak of "eyewitnesses" who testify or those in professional fields who give "*expert* testimony." When we refer to testimony in the legal system, we often mean the report given by one who has seen, heard or knows something relevant to the case at hand.

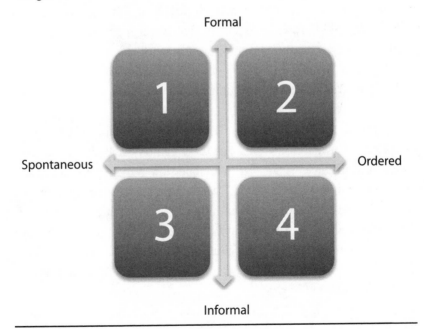

Figure 1.2

The second image is much like the scene I described above—a formal church service where an individual stands up and speaks extemporaneously. Both are pictures of this practice, but neither picture, even when considered together, provides a full picture of testifying.

When I speak of testifying, I am referring to a practice that is beyond extemporaneous speaking in a worship service. I have found it most helpful to envision an axis with four quadrants. These four quadrants represent four different ways in which a testimony might be delivered and received.[10]

Quadrant 1 represents the testifying scene I described at the start of this chapter. Someone offers a spontaneous testimony in a formal setting. It is the combination of these two that most often raises the anxiety of pastors. Not only is the door opened for anyone to say anything they want, they are given public and formal space to do so.

Quadrant 2 keeps the formal worship setting; however, the testimony shared is one that has been written out in advance. The stakes here are somewhat lowered. Although the anxiety of public speaking remains, there are few questions as to the content that is to be presented.

Directly beneath quadrant 2 is the fourth quadrant. Here the testimony has still been written in advance, but it is shared in a smaller setting—perhaps a small group or simply in an informal conversation with a friend over coffee. This fourth quadrant often feels the safest. The risk of public embarrassment is minimized, as is the anxiety of thinking up something to say.

Finally we come to quadrant 3. We are still in the informal setting of a small group or a conversation, but the testimony shared has not been planned in advance. An answer to the question "Where have you sensed the presence of the Lord this week?" would prompt a quadrant 3 testimony.

I will be referring to this graph multiple times throughout this book, particularly when we get to the final chapter of vision casting what this practice might look like in the church. I find it particularly helpful to keep this graph in mind if for no other reason than to expand limited understandings of this practice.

---

[10]For more on this, please see table 5.3, "Differentiating Between Kinds of Testimonies," found in chapter five.

Paul Ricoeur offers a broad definition of testimony that spans various contexts. Ricoeur defines it as "relating what one has seen or heard. The witness is the author of this action; it is he who, having seen or understood, makes a report of the event."[11] This report of the event, Ricoeur continues, is quasi-empirical, "because testimony is not perception itself but the report, that is, the story, the narration of an event. It consequently transfers things seen to the level of things said."[12] Imbedded in this definition is the understanding that testimony always contains some kind of interpretation.

Of course, what we are dealing with here is the most stripped down understanding of testimony, namely, reporting something you have seen or heard. When we speak of *religious* testimony, however, as we are with Jovhana's case, there are other elements to take into consideration. Here Ricoeur speaks of there being a "certain narrative kernel . . . preserved in strict union with the confession of faith. . . . A tension is thus created between confession of faith and narration of things seen."[13]

Homiletician Anna Carter Florence explains testimony as simply a narration of events paired with a confession of belief.[14] I am sympathetic to this definition with a brief caveat: initially, religious testimony may not include a confession of belief.[15] Many times, as was the case with the women at Jesus' tomb, we are able to articulate a narration of events but, for whatever reason, we are unable to attach a confession of belief. I know what I saw, but I do not know what it means and I am not able to ascribe belief to this event. It is in cases like these where we see the importance of Christian community. According to the apostle John, Mary was the first at the tomb on Easter morning, and upon finding it empty, she testifies to Peter and the other apostle: "They have taken the Lord out of the

---

[11]Paul Ricoeur, *Essays on Biblical Interpretation,* ed. Lewis Seymour Mudge (Philadelphia: Fortress, 1980), p. 123.

[12]Ibid.

[13]Ibid.

[14]Anna Carter Florence, *Preaching as Testimony* (Louisville, KY: Westminster John Knox Press, 2007), p. xiii.

[15]This is not necessarily a critique of Florence as she is primarily addressing preachers for whom a "confession of belief" is entirely appropriate and warranted. While her combination of narration and confession may be fitting for homileticians, I fear it places an unnecessary burden on the layperson that testifies.

tomb and we do not know where they have laid him" (Jn 20:2). It took various eyewitness reports, together with angelic announcements, to subscribe the confession of belief attached to the narrations that Jesus had risen. Mary was testifying to something before she was able to articulate the beliefs behind such events.

Simply put, a testimony is a narration of events seen or heard. *Religious* testimony often results in a confession of belief being tied to these narrated events. Again, to echo Ricoeur, it is important to remember that testimony is only quasi-empirical. Testimony is not the event itself; it is the *report* of that event.[16] We cannot go back in time and witness Jovhana's transforming moment at youth group. And even if we could, we still would not be privy to the thoughts and emotions coursing through her mind. For all we know, the lights were dim, the temperature was elevated and the entire experience was manufactured. If we are to believe that Jovhana experienced the love of God in a fresh way, we do so with her interpretation of the events. Her testimony is quasi-empirical. And it is testimonies like Jovhana's that have the potential to develop and deepen authentic Christian faith for adolescents.

This conviction stems from my own project, "Testimony and Formation," as well as studies in narrative psychology and sociology and theological convictions embedded in the practice of testifying, which I will address later. In the spring of 2007 I began "Testimony and Formation," a collection of interviews loosely guided by grounded theory on the relationship between testifying and adolescent spiritual formation.[17] Drawing from my holiness background in the Wesleyan church, I focused my attention on four Wesleyan churches in the Midwest that have made room for this practice of testifying within their youth

---

[16]Rebecca Chopp reminds us of the limitations of testimony: "I want to underscore the importance of respecting and protecting the gap between the named and the unnamable (a gap Christian theologians should know something about). We must resist sublating the gap by reducing it to the side of the event, and thus assuming that language will really represent the event (the modern dilemma) or that language is itself the event (certain postmodern theorists)" ("Theology and the Poetics of Testimony," *Criterion*, Winter 1998, p. 8).

[17]Grounded theory is a method of research that works in reverse of traditional social scientific methodology. Rather than beginning with a hypothesis, grounded theory is of a more emergent design where one's argument *emerges* from the compiled research. Kathy Charmaz's book *Constructing Grounded Theory: A Practical Guide Through Qualitative Anaylsis* (London: Sage Publications, 2006) has greatly guided my understanding of this method.

groups. Testifying has long been part of the holiness tradition, though for various reasons this practice has waned within the past few decades.[18] In keeping with a grounded theory approach, there is somewhat of an emergent design to my interviews in that, rather than coming into these interviews with a thesis to prove, the participants helped shape and influence the questions as well as the findings. In other words, my research is deeply embedded in their revelations. Of these four churches, two had designated times of testifying on a regular basis. These churches graciously allowed me to observe these testimony services and follow up with questions for both the testifier and those listening to the testimony.

It was clear from the start of this project that I would need to find a vocabulary that these teenagers could identify with. Many teenagers heard the word *testimony* and assumed I was asking about their conversion story. Some even had a memorized story of how they "became a Christian." Often in the project, I dropped the testimony language and instead asked these teenagers to tell me about a time when it seemed as if God was present in their lives. While different teenagers referred to testimonies by different names, it became clear in the course of this project that talking about God had a formative effect on their spiritual identities. The findings of these interviews are sprinkled throughout this book.

The practice of testifying is spiritually formative. Our deepest understandings of our religious identities are formed spiritually when we testify. *Spiritual formation* can be a kind of ecclesial buzzword, especially of late as language of Christian education is dwindling in some circles. That being the case let me clarify what I mean when I use the term *spiritual formation*. Drawing on various passages from the epistles, I understand spiritual formation to be the process in which one is transformed into like-mindedness with Jesus Christ while simultaneously resisting the pull to be formed into the mold of the world (Rom 12:2). How does this transformation take place? The apostle Peter offers a helpful, albeit lengthy, explanation of resisting the world and participating in the divine:

---

[18]I will discuss some of these reasons later in this book.

His divine power has given us everything we need for a godly life through our knowledge of him who called us by his own glory and goodness. Through these he has given us his very great and precious promises, so that through them you may participate in the divine nature, having escaped the corruption in the world caused by evil desires.

For this very reason, make every effort to add to your faith goodness; and to goodness, knowledge; and to knowledge, self-control; and to self-control, perseverance; and to perseverance, godliness; and to godliness, mutual affection; and to mutual affection, love. For if you possess these qualities in increasing measure, they will keep you from being ineffective and unproductive in your knowledge of our Lord Jesus Christ. (2 Pet 1:3-8 NIV)

Throughout this book I will be arguing for testifying as a practice that assists in the spiritual formation process. Articulating where we understand God to be present, along with how God interweaves his presence with our own spiritual narratives, affects and strengthens the knowledge we have, thereby aiding participation with the divine nature.

I should add that our richest understandings of spiritual formation are not limited to the field of theology, but take into account various theories from various fields. The heart of spiritual formation is rich and full and draws upon every aspect of the human experience—it is multi-dimensional and multi-layered. This project is an attempt to bring some of these disciplines together in a stratified way that helps us make more sense of this rich aspect of the Christian life.[19]

---

[19]Of course, any time you bring in multiple disciplines to explore a subject it is important to understand just how these various disciplines relate. What happens when various disciplines butt heads? How might these disciplines interact in a responsible way? Where do I locate myself on an interdisciplinary spectrum? Throughout this work I am assuming a stratified model of interdisciplinary work, meaning that I actively attempt to affirm the importance of various disciplines in describing different levels of reality. So in the case of my project, narrative psychology focuses on personal identity, which is subsequently strengthened by the social sciences. Sociology, on the other hand, works at the level of the group. I am focusing on a sociological theory that takes seriously the social construction of reality through human interaction and communal institutions. Theology focuses on the reality of God and the world in relation to God. It is important to note that none of these levels can be reduced to the other. Each has its own integrity and appropriate subject matters and methods. I accept sociological accounts of "reality" but do not believe they account for everything. For example, sociology might speak of a social construction of reality, including human understandings of God, but I want to place this in a theological framework where we acknowledge the active and formative presence of the triune God. For more on a stratified model of interdisciplinary work, please see Richard Osmer's book *Practical Theology: An Introduction* (Grand Rapids: Eerdmans, 2008), pp. 118-21.

This theological definition is brought into conversation with the social sciences, which I find immensely helpful in understanding the human dynamics of identity formation and the social construction of reality. While a practical theology of an articulacy theory of testimony has a great deal to gain from these intellectual resources, I believe that, ultimately, spiritual formation must appropriate them within a theological framework that speaks to the triune God and his self-disclosure to humanity.

So while I draw heavily from sociology—particularly understandings of social constructions of reality, which include human understandings of God—I want to place this understanding within a theological framework. In my case, the understanding of God's active presence in spiritual formation supports this framework. In other words, I accept sociological accounts but do not believe they account for everything. My understanding of revelation through Christ mediated by the Holy Spirit directly influences the way I engage with other fields.

In addition to this link between testifying and spiritual formation is an indelible link between narrative and identity. As has been stated by many others, narrative is more than just describing one's life; narrative also has a formative influence on one's life. Narrative does more than *describe*; it also *constructs*. What is more, this identity is further developed when one's narrative is articulated. An unspoken narrative might be formational for one's identity, but there is something about verbally articulating this narrative that holds a shaping force in one's spiritual identity. While human language does not make God's converting work a reality, human language may help an adolescent recognize where God is present and lay claim to it in her life, thereby enriching her faith. When she is able to recognize how God may have worked within her narrative and is able to articulate this occurrence, she is engaging in a theological practice that develops and deepens authentic Christian faith.

Narrative does more than *describe*; it also *constructs*.

This kind of narrative articulation concerning one's understandings of her religious experiences has a formative effect not only on her own perception of her spiritual identity but also on her community. While many of these narratives occur in community (we are not the only characters in our stories), these narratives also tend to call forth a communal response to confirm or challenge one's testimony. Testimonies given in this kind of communal setting strengthen the bonds of the community.

Ultimately, this book brings together two main bodies of literature: the history and theology of testimony as a Christian practice and social scientific understandings of narrative identities and articulation. Within the area of practical theology, testimony has been explored from various angles.[20] My project is particularly informed by practical theological reflections on testimony, specifically in the recent works of Kenda Creasy Dean, Thomas Long, Frank Roger Jr. and Anna Carter Florence. I am borrowing key insights from all of these scholars, but I am pushing their claims further in the direction of adolescent spiritual formation. It should be noted that, with exception of a single chapter by Kenda Dean, homileticians have done most of the work on testimony in practical theology.

Kenda Dean's chapter "Going Viral for Jesus: The Art of Testimony" in *Almost Christian: What the Faith of Our Teenagers Is Telling the American Church* deals exclusively with the relationship between testifying and moralistic therapeutic deism (as put forth by Christian Smith and Melinda Denton).[21] Dean explains how testimony solidifies the relationship

---

[20]We see various fields demonstrating differing perspectives on testimony. In the area of philosophy, C. A. J. Coady and Robert Audi discuss the epistemology of testifying. See C. A. J. Coady, *Testimony: A Philosophical Study* (Oxford: Clarendon, 1992); and Robert Audi, *Epistemology: A Contemporary Introduction to the Theory of Knowledge* (London: Routledge, 1998). Walter Brueggemann's *Theology of the Old Testament* is largely rooted on the concept of testimony. See Brueggemann, *Theology of the Old Testament: Testimony, Dispute, Advocacy* (Minneapolis: Fortress, 2005). Feminist theologians Rebecca Chopp and Mary McClintock Fulkerson have respectively published *The Power to Speak* and *Changing the Subject* concerning testimony as empowerment for the marginalized. See Rebecca Chopp, *The Power to Speak: Feminism, Language, God* (Eugene, OR: Wipf and Stock, 1991); Mary McClintock Fulkerson, *Changing the Subject: Women's Discourses and Feminist Theology* (Eugene, OR: Wipf and Stock, 2001). Historians, particularly those focusing on the holiness tradition, have explored the impact of testimony on the rise and development of the American holiness movement as well as the emergence of various revivals. See Donald Dayton, *Discovering an Evangelical Heritage* (Peabody, MA: Hendrickson, 1988); Melvin E. Dieter, *The Holiness Revival of the Nineteenth Century* (Lanham, MD: Scarecrow Press, 1996). As mentioned earlier, Paul Ricoeur has been a leading figure in the area of hermeneutics; and Anna Carter Florence has explored the subject from the perspective of hermeneutical theory and formation of the homiletician.

[21]Kenda Creasy Dean, *Almost Christian: What the Faith of Our Teenagers Is Telling the American Church* (New York: Oxford University Press, 2010), pp. 131-56; Christian Smith and Melinda Lundquist Denton, *Soul Searching: The Religious and Spiritual Lives of American Teenagers* (Oxford: Oxford University Press, 2005), p. 131.

between the adolescent and the greater congregation in a way that shapes and informs the adolescent's Christian identity. I am very sympathetic to Dean's work and wish to take her research further by going deeper into theories of sociological understandings of articulacy in order to identify the necessity of speaking of faith, and to put the practice of testimony in dialogue with developed theologies of testifying.[22]

Thomas Long's book *Testimony: Talking Ourselves into Being Christian* also holds similarities with my project. Long proposes that when we verbalize our faith, it has a spiritually formative effect—the more we talk about our faith, the more faithful we become.[23] However, it should be noted that this book is intended for a popular audience with no theological or social theory explicit within his writings. What is more, this book does not address the specific problem of faith articulacy for adolescents.

Frank Roger Jr. nods in the direction of my project with his recently published book, *Finding God in the Graffiti: Empowering Teenagers Through Stories*. Roger's project overlaps with mine in that both of us see the significance of the concept of narrative in the spiritual formation of teenagers. Our emphases differ, however, as Roger focuses on the made-up narratives constructed in the imaginations of his teenagers. I, on the other hand, am looking for autobiographical, testimonial accounts of one's narrative.[24]

While these projects offer substantial contributions to the topic of testimony and spiritual formation, I am hoping to push their research further in terms of bringing testimony into conversation with sociological understandings of articulacy and adolescent faith development in greater length and detail. This task can be broken up into four additional chapters.

Chapter Two: Faithful Words Prompt Faithful "Reality." My interest in the call to nurture the practice of testimony is preceded by the Na-

---

[22]Dean, *Almost Christian*, pp. 131-56.

[23]Long, *Testimony*.

[24]Frank Rogers Jr., *Finding God in the Graffiti: Empowering Teenagers Through Stories* (Cleveland, OH: Pilgrim Press: 2011). Rogers's book makes a significant contribution to the field of youth ministry as he explores ways of sanctifying imaginations in a way that spiritually forms an individual. While his work appeals to a broad audience, he is primarily interested in reaching teenagers considered "at risk."

tional Study of Youth and Religion (NSYR), the results of which are published in *Soul Searching: The Religious and Spiritual Lives of American Teenagers* by Christian Smith and Melinda Lundquist Denton. Between 2002 and 2003 the NSYR conducted 3,290 surveys and 167 in-depth phone interviews. The study found that, with exception of Mormons and some conservative evangelicals, the vast majority of teenagers were unable to talk about their faith, beliefs and religious practices, and why any of this mattered to them.[25] What this study suggests is that (a) religion is unimportant to North American teenagers, (b) the church has been woefully inadequate in teaching Christian beliefs, or (c) at the very least, the church has been inadequate in passing on a language for adolescents to speak of what they have been taught.

Embedded in this study is the idea that, while teenagers claim religion—and more specifically, *Christian* religion—to be important in their lives, few are able to articulate a basic understanding of Christian faith. While there are exceptions to this assertion, many adolescents are vastly inarticulate on basic tenets of Christian faith.[26] Drawing from philosopher and social theorist Charles Taylor, Smith and Denton warn that an inability to speak of one's faith makes the plausibility of maintaining this faith tenuous.

Using the research found in the NSYR I will show the problematic implications of religious inarticulacy, particularly when it comes to one's understanding of reality. Articulation aids in increased reality maintenance. For better or worse, the more you talk about something the easier time you will have believing it is true. Drawing from Berger and Luckmann's *Social Construction of Reality*, I will show the richness that comes with the ability to articulate one's understanding of faith.

Chapter Three: What We Say Is What We Are: Articulating Identity Through Narrative. This chapter focuses on the indelible link between narrative and identity. I undertake the task of showing how narrative not only *describes* one's life but also plays a prescriptive role in actually *shaping* one's life and identity. Here I draw from various aspects of the

---

[25]Smith and Denton, *Soul Searching*, p. 131.

[26]It should be noted that the testimonies I encountered and am encouraging are not simply statements of faith; rather, these are personal narratives that often have basic tenets of faith embedded within the narrative, either explicitly or implicitly.

social sciences, namely, narrative psychology and sociology to show the necessity of a coherent narrative undergirding one's sense of identity as is commonly understood today. Without the ability to recall a coherent narrative, trauma ensues. As I transition to the shaping role of narratives on the wider religious community, I continue to draw from the afore-mentioned social sciences in addition to findings from a neuroscientific perspective focusing on the importance of community in order to process and interpret various narratives.

Neglecting to articulate one's narrative does not necessarily make that narrative less formative; likewise, articulating one's narrative does not guarantee certain spiritual formation results. Nevertheless, within this chapter I argue that articulating one's spiritual narrative actually does something within an individual as well as the community to which this individual belongs. The act of making a verbal statement carries with it something concrete that alters one's understanding of self and the community in which she or he belongs.

Chapter Four: A Theology of Testimony. As mentioned earlier, most of the writing on religious testimony focuses on the practice of testimony within ecclesial settings. Ricoeur offers a somewhat more theoretical approach as he addresses the role and warrants of testimony in religious contexts. Very little, however, has been written on theological rationales for testifying in the first place. The anomaly to this claim is Phoebe Palmer, a nineteenth-century holiness evangelist and writer who understood testifying to be an indispensable aspect of Christian faith. While Palmer does not systematically lay out a theological rationale for this practice, she does provide a kind of framework from which we can understand how crucial this practice is in Christian faith. The theological framework found within her writings will guide much of my own theological assessment. Palmer's writings and teachings on testimony are by no means comprehensive, and I will bring her work in conversation with Karl Barth's understanding of *Zeugnis,* which we translate as "testimony" or "witness." The rationale behind this seemingly strange pairing of conversation partners will also be addressed in this chapter.

Chapter Five: Testimony in Practice: Toward a Practical Theology. I conclude my project by suggesting a pragmatic approach to responsibly practicing testimony with North American adolescents. Drawing from earlier reported research and addressing common concerns, I propose a way of testifying that will allow adolescents to tap into and articulate their understanding of how God has been at work in their lives.

It should be noted that in addition to sprinkling in findings from my earlier project, "Testimony and Formation," I will also address various objections and hindrances to this practice, which certainly deserve our attention.

Testifying is a rich, spiritually formative practice. Testimonies might look different depending on one's location. In my own experience, testifying has taken on different forms throughout the past twenty-five years. One's testimony can be spontaneous or ordered, it can be in a formal or informal setting, and this testimony can be live or edited, given by a lone speaker or with another individual in an interview format. Regardless of what form the testimony takes, articulating where we understand God to be at work within our life is a powerful form of spiritual formation.

2

Faithful Words Prompt
Faithful "Reality"

Soon after we were married, my husband returned home from a trip away and commented on the cleanliness of our four-hundred-square-foot apartment. "Did you spend time cleaning?" he asked.

I told him that I hadn't. I had, however, "kept the curtains drawn while he was away so that the dust wouldn't get in."

The minute the words were out of mouth I knew my logic was faulty. Though that logic seems laughable to me as an adult, since it remained in my mind, unspoken and unchallenged, it stayed there dormant until its debut following my husband's trip. Of course the sun doesn't cause dust to come streaming through the window—it merely highlights the floating dust particles already present. I was not even aware that childhood logic still remained in my subconscious until I said it out loud.

> We have a hard time finding legitimacy to our beliefs if we are unable to talk about our beliefs.

Sometimes we don't know what we really think until we say it out loud. We often talk our way into our beliefs. We have a hard time finding legitimacy in our beliefs if we are unable to talk about them. Often we hold on to hidden beliefs, opinions and feelings that are only made accessible to us after we verbalize them. That which remains unspoken is often murky, opaque and of little acknowledged value to our everyday lives.

> That which remains unspoken is often murky, opaque and of little acknowledged value to our everyday lives.

The concern with adolescent faith development is not that they are speaking incorrectly of God; it's that they are seldom speaking of God at all. And even when they are asked to vaguely artic-ulate their religious beliefs, many are still speechless.

The fact that Jovhana was able to articulately express her religious beliefs is an anomaly for North American teenagers today. When asked what specific beliefs they held, many of the teenagers interviewed in the NSYR gave the following responses:

"Um, I haven't really thought about that. [pause] I don't know."

"Just like, um, what they taught me, what I grew up knowing, I don't know."

"I believe in the [pause], I, ohhh [pause], I don't think I'd really like to talk about that."

"I don't remember."

"I don't think so right now."

"Hm, I don't know, I'd have to like ask somebody or something, I don't know."

"Um, I guess I believe . . . [laughs], um, I don't really know. I don't really know how to answer it."[1]

Within the NSYR, Smith and Denton found the "vast majority" of US teenagers interviewed "to be incredibly inarticulate about their faith, their religious beliefs and practices and its meaning or place in their lives." Smith and Denton concede they expect such answers from nonreligious teenagers, but many of these answers came from self-described religious teenagers: "A substantial minority of religiously affiliated U.S. teenagers, when asked if they held any specific religious beliefs, simply answered, 'No,' or, 'Not really,' or, 'Not that I can think of.'" They describe another "large minority [who] did claim to hold religious beliefs but were unable to describe them."[2]

This kind of inarticulacy was found not only among self-described religious teenagers, it was also prevalent among those self-described re-ligious teenagers who regularly attended church. The following conver-

---

[1]Christian Smith and Melinda Lundquist Denton, *Soul Searching: The Religious and Spiritual Lives of American Teenagers* (Oxford: Oxford University Press, 2005), p. 131.
[2]Ibid.

sation took place between an interviewer and a fifteen-year-old white, mainline Methodist girl who regularly attended two Sunday services, youth group and a Wednesday night Bible study. When asked what she believed, she responded:

> T: [Pause] I don't really know how to answer that.

> I: Are there any beliefs at all that are important to you? Really generally.

> T: [Pause] I don't know.

> I: Take your time if you want.

> T: I think that you should just, if you're gonna do something wrong then you should always ask for forgiveness and he's gonna forgive you no matter what, 'cause he gave up his only son to take all the sins for you . . .[3]

Despite these high levels of inarticulacy, Jovhana's testimony illustrates that there are those who are able to articulate their faith. Furthermore, I believe Jovhana's words of faith help create for her a more realistic faith. Smith and Denton conclude: "Religiously devoted teenagers were more articulate than nominally religious teens, for obvious reasons."[4] Most of these "religiously devoted teenagers" were from evangelical or Mormon backgrounds.[5] Mainline Protestant teenagers, however, were among the least articulate.[6] And while older teenagers tended to be slightly more articulate than younger teenagers, it was not by much. They write, "Impressively articulate teens were few and far between. The vast majority simply could not express themselves on matters of God, faith, religion, or spiritual life."[7]

---

[3]Ibid., p. 132.
[4]Ibid., p. 133. Dean provides a table describing religiously devoted teenagers according to the NSYR. Religiously devoted youth made up 8 percent of those interviewed. Characteristics include the following: (1) "attends religious services weekly or more," (2) "faith is very or extremely important in everyday life," (3) "feels very or extremely close to God," (4) "currently involved in a religious youth group," (5) "prays a few times a week or more" and (6) "reads scripture once or twice a week or more." Kenda Creasy Dean, *Almost Christian: What the Faith of Our Teenagers Is Telling the American Church* (New York: Oxford University Press, 2010), p. 41.
[5]I will discuss these groups in the following chapter.
[6]Smith and Denton, *Soul Searching*, p. 131.
[7]Ibid., p. 133.

Smith and Denton hypothesize that this inarticulacy may be due to a lack of education on the matter and/or the lack of opportunities to practice what has been taught. They explain: "We do not believe that teenage inarticulacy about religious matters reflects any general teen incapacity to think and speak well."[8] This assertion is based on their finding that teenagers appeared to be quite articulate on matters in which they had been educated—even personal matters such as sex or drugs.[9] "Our impression as interviewers," they continue:

> was that many teenagers could not articulate matters of faith because they have not been effectively educated in and provided opportunities to practice talking about their faith. Indeed, it was our distinct sense that for many of the teens we interviewed, *our interview was the first time that any adult had ever asked them what they believed and how it mattered in their lives.*[10]

Smith and Denton are quite clear on their findings: many teenagers who claim a religious identity—particularly a Christian religious identity—are unable to adequately articulate the basic beliefs they claim are important to them.

Smith and Denton make the assertion that we acquire religious language much in the same way we learn to speak any other kind of language.[11] First, we need regular exposure to native speakers using this new kind of language. Second, we need plenty of practice to speak it ourselves. Smith and Denton conclude: "Many U.S. teenagers, it appears, are not getting a significant amount of such exposure and practice and so are simply not learning the religious language of their faith tradition."[12]

Instead, they assert, the majority of North American teenagers today are practicing a kind of moralistic therapeutic deism (MTD).[13] What has

---

[8]Ibid.

[9]Ibid., p. 33.

[10]Ibid.

[11]I will discuss language acquisition in more in chapter five.

[12]Ibid.

[13]Smith and Denton identify the creed of MTD as follows: (1) A God exists who created and orders the world and watches over human life on earth. (2) God wants people to be good, nice, and fair to each other, as taught in the Bible and by most world religions. (3) The central goal of life is to be happy and to feel good about oneself. (4) God does not need to be particularly involved in one's life except when God is needed to resolve a problem. (5) Good people go to heaven when they die. Ibid., pp. 162-63.

traditionally been understood as foundational to basic Christian faith has been supplanted by an instrumentalist view of religion. "Most instinctively suppose," Smith and Denton explain, "that religion exists to help individuals be and do what they want, and not as an external tradition or authority or divinity that makes compelling claims and demands on their lives, especially to change or grow in ways they may not immediately want to."[14] Religion makes us feel good. It solves problems. "God is treated as something like a cosmic therapist, or counselor, a ready and competent helper who responds in terms of trouble but who does not particularly ask for devotion or obedience."[15] Operating from an MTD perspective, a teenager assumes "that central to living a good and happy life is being a good, moral person. That means being nice, kind, pleasant, respectful, responsible, at work on self-improvement, taking care of one's health, and doing one's best to be successful."[16] Concepts such as sin, holiness, justification, the Eucharist and church are replaced with niceness, happiness and merit-based heavenly rewards.

REACTIONS TO THE NSYR

Before making any connections between the NSYR findings on inarticulacy and the practice of testimony, it is necessary to pause and address some of the questions and concerns that have risen regarding the study. It has solicited a number of critical reactions from the public. The majority of these critiques seem to fall into one of two categories. Some are critical of the effectiveness of the methods used to elicit the data. Others are more critical of how the data is interpreted. Both critiques deserve careful attention.

Critique 1: Effectiveness of NSYR's methodology. Many of the critiques revolve around the effectiveness of the methods used to obtain the answers. Some argue the interviewers were asking too much of their interviewees. After all, they are just teenagers. Smith and Denton address this issue, claiming that while they did not expect adolescents "to be sophisticated theologians," very few of the Christian teenagers were able to even "come close to representing marginally coherent accounts of the

---

[14]Ibid., pp. 147-48.
[15]Ibid., p. 148.
[16]Ibid., p. 163.

basic, important religious beliefs of their own faith traditions."[17]

It is possible that what was seen as a teenager's inability to speak of her faith may, in fact, simply be reticence. Smith and Denton admit that many of the teenagers interviewed thought speaking publicly of their faith was illegal.[18] However, this still does not change the fact that these religious responses were expressly requested and welcomed by the interviewers.

Others might argue this inarticulacy is simply the plight of the adolescent brain—as if teenagers are incapable of speaking articulately on *any* subject. However, many of the NSYR interviews indicate that teenagers are very articulate on certain subjects—even very personal subjects that they have been educated on and given opportunities to practice speaking about; hence their fluidity on topics concerning drug abuse and sexually transmitted diseases.[19]

Perhaps the strongest critique comes from Jeffrey Stout's concerns regarding the effectiveness of interview methods in general. While his critiques are not directed toward the NSYR, his concerns should nevertheless be addressed.

In his article "Liberal Society and the Language of Morals," Stout voices disagreement toward those who think an individual's life commitments must be grounded in some kind of "philosophical foundation or purpose of life."[20] This lack of a foundation, some say, simultaneously results in a lack of "language to explain" life-defining commitments. The language to justify commitments in one's life is not found in a philosophical foundation that is accessed through interview questions, Stout explains; rather, "It rests in the details of the story. It is by telling [a] story and implicitly invoking its evaluative framework that [one] initially understands [one's] life and justifies [one's] current commitments as superior to [one's] old ones."[21] I find Stout's arguments convincing and will expand on his words later in this chapter.

Kenda Creasy Dean was one of the face-to-face interviewers for the NSYR and has since helped interpret these findings for the church. She

---

[17]Ibid., p. 137.

[18]Dean, *Almost Christian*, p. 135.

[19]Ibid., p. 133.

[20]Jeffrey Stout, "Liberal Society and the Language of Morals," *Soundings* 69 (1986): 37.

[21]Ibid., p. 37.

admits, "Interviews can be unreliable methods for unearthing deep commitments; our most cherished convictions surface more naturally in stories than in propositional answers to interview questions."[22] There is a "hitch," however. Dean continues:

> If we assume that teenagers did not represent themselves accurately when answering questions about religion in the NSYR, then we must also assume that they did not represent themselves accurately in questions about families, relationships, future plans, and other subjects they cared about. Furthermore, since interviews are the most common means of obtaining qualitative research, to invalidate teenagers' responses in the NSYR would call into question most sociological research on adolescents.[23]

In addition to this "hitch," the NSYR was very clear on its commitment to using "standard mixed method research principles to maximize reliability (i.e., multiple conversations, culturally matched interviewers, alternate phrasing, etc.)."[24]

Critique 2: Interpreting the results. It is not just the effectiveness of the NSYR's methodology that has been called into question; many practical theologians have questioned whether or not this moralistic therapeutic deism should be all that worrisome to the church. And even if practical theologians agree MTD is a problem, the question still remains whether or not inarticulacy is a contributing factor.

"What is wrong with moralistic therapeutic deism?" some might ask. "What does it matter whether or not a teenager can articulate her beliefs?" "So what if basic Christian beliefs are replaced with MTD? Isn't this better than nothing?" "If MTD makes kids happy, caring and adjusted members of society is that not a good thing?"

Those operating from a humanist perspective or who see Jesus as simply a moral exemplar may be satisfied with these findings. An MTD philosophy fosters a kind of niceness and respectfulness that many would love to see in the foundation of the moral character of North American youth. Addressing this concern, Dean remarks, "Some would argue . . . that Moralistic Therapeutic Deism is not worth such a fuss. History has seen worse

---

[22]Dean, *Almost Christian*, pp. 34-35.
[23]Ibid., p. 35.
[24]Ibid., p. 222n19.

heresies. We want young people to be happy and feel good about themselves; it is good to help people get along."[25] And yet there is a consumerist bent within MTD that does not line up with the missional, sacrificial core of the gospel. Speaking of "wasteful love" and self-sacrifice, Dean reminds us what life looks like when our lives are woven into the life of Jesus Christ.[26] The Holy Spirit empowers us to participate in the life of God. We rejoice where God rejoices. We suffer where God suffers. Our very understanding of what it means to bear witness comes from the Greek *marturia,* or martyr. To participate in the life of God means to bear witness to the love and suffering of the Godhead. The gospel is more than niceness and happiness; there are deep roots of suffering and forbearance that are integral to our identity as Christians. Christianity is a call for self-giving, whereas MTD can be considered "a religion aimed at self-fulfillment."[27] The tenets of MTD may be fine as characteristics of another religion, but these tenets are not at the heart of Christianity.[28]

While religious inarticulacy does not imply inactivity on the part of the Holy Spirit, it does substantially limit the learner's ability to both appropriate Christian tradition and access this tradition in a meaningful way.

This is an alarming study for those who long to see teenagers participate in the life of God. Jesus is more than an exemplary figure or a cosmic therapist, and spirituality is more than something designed to make us feel good. If we believe the salvific work of God matters and affects us in this life and the one to come, the findings in this study warrant serious attention. While religious inarticulacy does not imply inactivity on the part of the Holy Spirit, it does substantially limit the learner's ability to both appropriate Christian tradition and access this tradition in a meaningful way.

Other critiques of the NSYR revolve around the idea that we cannot assess adolescents' faith by whether or not they can talk about it. Some

---

[25]Ibid., p. 85.
[26]Ibid., p. 88.
[27]Ibid., p. 104.
[28]Ibid., p. 198.

argue that Smith and Denton's idea of what constitutes Christian belief is too cognitive. In her book *Everyday Religion*, Nancy Ammerman of Boston University claims that we know and experience faith as "fragments," "side plots" and "tangents," not as dogmatic statements. She explains: "A person may recognize moral imperatives that have a transcendent grounding without ever having a 'religious experience' or being able to articulate a set of doctrines about God."[29] While I do not argue with the truth of this statement, I see this as more descriptive than normative. Recognizing a moral imperative, as good as that may be in itself, is not a substitute for vibrant faith. While it may be good, I am not sure it is good *enough*. I want more than the recognition of a moral imperative; I want both the recognition and the articulation of the *wellspring* of this moral imperative. There is immense pedagogical value in the ability to articulate where one sees the presence of God. This articulation is crucial in the establishment of a deep understanding of one's spiritual identity.

James K. A. Smith of Calvin College echoes Ammerman and offers the critique that many rely too much on the cognitive as opposed to affective understandings of faith. A critique could be made that Christian Smith is speaking of faith too cognitively with a "reductionistic account that fails to honor the richness and complexity of the human person."[30] James K. A. Smith explains that we often find ourselves believing something before we are able to express it in an articulate thought. He goes on to clarify:

> Before we can offer our rational explanations of the world, we have already assumed a whole constellation of beliefs—a *worldview*—that governs and conditions our perceptions of the world. Our primordial orientation or comportment to the world is not as thinkers but as believers. Beliefs, we might say, are more "basic" than ideas.[31]

We are defined not by what we think, he explains, nor by "the set of ideas we assent to—but rather what we believe, the commitments and trusts that orient our being-in-the-world. This moves the essence of the human

---

[29]Nancy Ammerman, *Everyday Religion: Observing Modern Religious Lives* (Oxford: Oxford University Press, 2007), p. 226. Thanks to Jeff Keuss for pointing me in this direction.

[30]James K. A. Smith, *Desiring the Kingdom: Worship, Worldview, and Cultural Formation* (Grand Rapids: Baker Academic, 2009), p. 43. Thanks to Jeff Keuss for pointing me in the direction of Smith.

[31]Ibid.

person from the more abstract, disembodied word of ideas to a pre-rational level of commitments that are more ingrained in the human person."[32] He concludes, "Before we are thinkers, we are believers."[33]

While I appreciate this call to give increased importance to the affective, I am somewhat leery of Smith's dichotomy between believing and thinking, as if the two can be neatly separated. And even if this dichotomy was established, I cannot help but wonder what benefits would arise when beliefs and thinking align in such a way that both can be articulated. Even if teenagers are stuck gazing at this "constellation of beliefs" in a non-cognitive, inarticulate way, what might they gain by being given adequate words to name and describe these constellations? Star-gazing is a richer experience when we recognize and name the pictures and stories we see.

Star-gazing is a richer experience when we recognize and name the pictures and stories we see.

Further, both Ammerman and Smith are speaking out against a faith that is reduced to theological assertions to which one merely assents or recites. The kind of faith I am speaking of goes beyond doctrinal statements one can recite to a kind of lived faith where one is able to see and articulate God's action in the present world.

I agree with these critiques in that I do not think it determinative of one's faith to be able to regurgitate the Heidelberg Catechism and provide subsequent commentary (though I would certainly welcome attempts to do so). And it is at this point where I find myself wanting to nudge Christian Smith further. I am not as concerned as Smith about what theological assertions can be made. My desire is not so much for teenagers to be able to clearly articulate beliefs; rather, I want them to be able to articulate a story—some kind of narrative where they understand God's story to intersect their own story. I have no desire to argue for mere repetition of orthodox, dogmatic assertions. My understanding of articulating beliefs takes on a more organic form than what has been described above. Taking Stout's insight into consideration, that sometimes our deepest truths are embedded within narratives, I argue for providing the language, space and opportunity

[32]Ibid.
[33]Ibid.

for teenagers to testify where they understand God to be at work in their own narratives, acknowledging that religious beliefs will be present within these narratives, both explicitly and implicitly. So while a teenager may not be able to offer an articulated response regarding God's interaction with the world, it is quite possible that a testimony of hers would shed light on where and how she understands God to be at work. Take, for example, the testimony presented by Jovhana in the opening chapter. While her testimony is not fraught with theological terminology, implicit within her story are her beliefs concerning the atonement, God's love and what it means to be a Christian. Jovhana expressed a robust pneumatology of a Spirit that breaks into our everyday lives and has transforming power. She said a great deal in her short testimony—more than she realized.

I want teenagers to be able to articulate their faith not in order to determine whether or not they are orthodox Christians, but because I understand this kind of articulation as formative for the spiritual identity of the teenager. An articulate faith has the potential for a positive effect on one's spiritual identity. Articulation nurtures faith and holds pedagogical value in the spiritual formation of adolescents. I am not arguing that articulation makes one's faith more authentic or more valid; rather, my argument revolves around a sociological understanding of articulation as a means of fostering reality. Faith is not necessarily more real when one can speak of it, but articulation does contribute toward one's understanding of subjective reality.[34] The practice of testifying utilizes the "vocabularies, grammars, stories and key messages of faith" that can help adolescents deepen authentic faith.[35] While human language does not make God's converting work a reality, it may help adolescents recognize where God is present and lay claim to it in their life, thereby enriching their faith. While a testimony alone is not what makes faith

---

[34]I will explain what I mean by "reality" later in this chapter.

[35]Christian Smith, "Is Moralistic Therapeutic Deism the New Religion of American Youth? Implications for the Challenge of Religious Socialization and Reproduction," in *Passing on the Faith: Transforming Traditions for the Next Generation of Jews, Christians and Muslims,* ed. James Heft (New York: Fordham University Press, 2006), p. 70. Smith borrows much of this logic from various works of Charles Taylor: *Sources of the Self: The Making of Modern Identity* (Cambridge, MA: Harvard University Press, 1989), and "Self-Interpreting Animals," in *Human Agency and Language* (Cambridge: Cambridge University Press, 1985), pp. 45-76.

plausible, this practice holds pedagogical value in the spiritual development of adolescents.

THE RELATIONSHIP BETWEEN WHAT WE SAY AND WHAT WE BELIEVE

Why this stress on articulation? Why not allow a teenager's experience or "worldview" to simply remain pre-linguistic? Does it matter whether or not a teenager can provide the articulation for what James K. A. Smith might call more affective beliefs?

Various sociological studies have linked the connection between articulation and "reality maintenance."[36] *If we want something to seem "real" to us, we must be able to talk about it. We will have a difficult time maintaining Christian faith if we are unable to talk about this faith.* Making a similar claim, Christian Smith argues that inarticulacy undermines the plausibility of faith and that "religious faith, practice, and commitment can be no more than indistinctly real when people cannot talk much about them. In other words, articulacy fosters reality."[37] I operate under a more nuanced understanding of this bold claim: my Wesleyan tradition insists that divine grace is at work in us even before we have words to describe it. However, language helps us recognize and lay claim to what God is doing in us.

That is not to say that justification comes through *articulated* faith alone. I am not suggesting that if people cannot verbally express their faith then it is not real. I am, however, in agreement with sociological understandings that articulacy fosters reality as argued by Peter Berger and Thomas Luckmann in their book *Social Constructivism*.

The subject of social constructivism has exploded since Berger and Luckmann's 1966 seminal book. According to Christian Smith, however, much of the work done on social constructivism since that time has run amok.[38] Throughout the past few decades social constructivism has been

---

[36]For example, consider "persuasion theory" as explained by Herbert Simons and Jean Jones. Herbert W. Simons, Joanne Morreale and Bruce E. Gronbeck, *Persuasion in Society* (Thousand Oaks, CA: Sage Publications, 2001).

[37]Smith, "Is Moralistic Therapeutic Deism the New Religion?"

[38]Christian Smith, *What Is a Person? Rethinking Humanity, Social Life, and the Moral Good from the Person Up* (Chicago: University of Chicago Press, 2010), p. 121.

influenced by various schools of thought (Smith points to poststructuralism and postmodernism) and runs the risk of being warped by "intellectual naiveté, half truths, rhetorical hyperbole, trendy external influence, and the scholarly rigor mortis that can set in as new, invigorating perspectives age into formulaic guild research programs."[39]

Smith explains that social constructivism today comes in both weak and strong versions. Whether we understand social constructivism in the weak or strong sense will greatly affect our sociological understanding of the relationship between language and reality. The weak version of social constructionism acknowledges:

> All human knowledge is conceptually mediated and can be and usually is influenced by particular and contingent sociocultural factors such as material interests, group structures, linguistic categories, technological development, and the like—such that what people believe to be real is significantly shaped not only by objective reality but also by their sociocultural contexts.[40]

In other words, what I think is real consists of a combination of what is truly, objectively real outside of myself, as well as what my social context leads me to believe is real (whether or not it truly is real). While my social context may greatly assist in my understanding of reality, there is also a kind of reality that exists separately and independently of my own consciousness and context.

Strong social constructivism, however, makes a much bolder claim. Smith explains:

> Reality itself for humans is a human, social construction, constituted by human mental categories, discursive practices, definitions of situations, and symbolic exchanges that are sustained as "real" through ongoing social interactions that are in turn shaped by particular interests, perspectives, and, usually, imbalances of power—our knowledge about reality is therefore entirely culturally relative, since no human has access to reality "as it really is" (if such a thing exists or can be talked about intelligibly) because we can never escape our human epistemological and linguistic limits to verify whether our beliefs about reality correspond with externally objective reality.[41]

---

[39]Ibid.
[40]Ibid., pp. 121-22.
[41]Ibid., p. 122.

In other words, humans construct all that is seen as real.

Though the term initially appears pejorative, I operate under a "weak" understanding of social constructivism. While I believe there is a God that is beyond my social construction, I acknowledge that much of my understanding of God is shaped by my social context. What I believe I know about God is not the same thing as God in God's essence.

This is in line with Berger and Luckmann's work that clearly states their "specific concern was not epistemology or metaphysics, but the sociology of knowledge."[42] Smith goes on to explain, "Never did Berger and Luckmann conflate human knowledge about reality with reality itself or claim that the content of beliefs was entirely dependent on social processes."[43]

When I speak of articulation fostering social constructionism, I am using reality in the weak sense of the term. Articulation fosters a subjective or, as Smith would say, a weak social construction. Articulation holds substantial sway over perceived reality.[44]

> **While articulation may not affect my status before God, it may affect the way I *understand* God to be at work in my life and subsequently how I *respond* to God.**

Why does this distinction between strong and weak versions of social constructivism matter? *An ability to articulate faith does not create an objective reality, nor does an inability to articulate faith indicate a faithless reality.* While articulation may not affect my status before God, it may affect the way I *understand* God to be at work in my life and subsequently how I *respond* to God. Though human language does not make God's converting work a reality, it may help adolescents recognize where God is present and lay claim to it in their life, thereby enriching their faith.

---

[42]Ibid., p. 126.

[43]Ibid. In fact, to differentiate between reality and people's beliefs about reality, Berger and Luckmann put quotation marks around "reality" and "knowledge" at the beginning of their book. They explain, however, that to continue using these quotation marks "would be stylistically awkward," hence they discontinue the practice. Peter L. Berger and Thomas Luckmann, *The Social Construction of Reality: A Treatise in the Sociology of Knowledge* (Garden City, NY: Doubleday, 1966), p. 2.

[44]Though I am using *reality* in the weak sense, I will not use quotation marks each time I use the word.

How Articulation Affects "Reality": An Articulacy Theory of Testimony

These strong statements beg the question, "How?" *How* does articulation foster "reality"? *How* can articulation help us recognize where God might be at work in our lives? *How* might articulation nurture the faith and spiritual identity of North American youth?

Articulation does more than describe. Under the proper conditions, a few uttered words quite literally change reality. In his 1955 seminal Harvard lectures, J. L. Austin asserts that within certain parameters, "to *say* something is to *do* something."[45] Austin most notably points to the marriage act, where the spoken word in the proper context creates the reality of a legal bond between two people.[46] Our society depends upon "speech acts" of this kind; hence the swearing in of Lyndon B. Johnson roughly two hours after the assassination of John F. Kennedy. The haste that necessitated Johnson's swearing in elevated the supremacy of words over other important factors. This oath was made not on the steps of the Capitol but in *Air Force One* on Texan soil. The oath was not administered by the chief justice but by a federal judge who happened to be nearby. In the end, it was not pomp and circumstance that made Lyndon B. Johnson president on November 22, 1963; it was *words*. Words do more than describe. Under the proper circumstances, *words create*.

On April 16, 2001, I told my husband-to-be, John, that I loved him. We were sitting on a couch in a small room in our church and I said those three words out loud for the first time. I had loved John for a long time before I articulated the sentiment. Prior to this declaration my actions showed evidence of this love. But saying the words out loud was a game-changer in our relationship. It was not enough that I *felt* love for John. It did not matter as much that I *acted* lovingly toward John. Once the words were actually said out loud the relationship moved forward. Saying the words out loud changed something about our relationship.

Or consider the phrase, "I'm sorry." I might feel sorry. I might act sorry. But there is something about saying the words out loud to another

---

[45]J. L. Austin, *How to Do Things with Words* (Cambridge, MA: Harvard University Press, 1975), p. 12.
[46]Ibid., pp. 1-11.

person that opens the door further for a reconciled relationship.

Articulation does more than describe. Were I to articulate my basic Christian beliefs, my words would be more than mere description. In speaking, I am also given access to my beliefs in a new way that has the potential to define how I understand my faith and my relationship to that faith.[47]

Berger and Luckmann explain that in the midst of a conversation, my speaking provides my conversation partner insight into my thought. I become available to her. Within this conversation we have "reciprocal access to our two subjectivities."[48] But she is not the only one who gleans something from this verbal interaction. At the same time she is hearing me speak, *I am also hearing myself speak*. This is commonly experienced when a person expresses a particular sentiment only to follow it up with something along the lines of, "Wow, that sounded a lot better in my head." Berger and Luckmann explain: "My own being becomes massively and continuously available to myself at the same time that it is so available [to her]. . . . Language makes 'more real' my subjectivity not only to my conversation partner but also myself."[49] Berger and Luckmann assert that people must talk about themselves in order to know themselves.[50]

A church where I was pastoring was preparing for its annual youth Sunday, where the teenagers would lead the entire service. It was fairly easy finding volunteers to sing or take offering or perform a skit. Finding people to preach or speak publicly of their faith was a different matter.

---

[47]In the interview with my father, Paul Hontz, mentioned at the beginning of this book, I saw him gesturing to this effect: "There's something about externalizing it. And I think speaking the words—I think—I don't know how to explain it, but I intuit that there is something very, very powerful about the spoken word. I think you could almost develop a whole theology about that. Even when a person takes a vow. . . . You take your marriage vows and there is something about articulating, 'I do,' 'I will,' 'For better for worse,' that has a way of crystallizing, making more concrete the internal sentiment that happens. Plus I think one of the things that goes along with that is when we voice something—when we give witness to something—we allow people to bear witness to the commitment that we've made or the stance that we've made. . . . And so I think it raises our own level of accountability. I think there's something in the Scripture that speaks to the . . . 'and declares with his mouth that Jesus is Lord.' . . . I think there's something very important about that. Almost something mystical and spiritual that transpires there." Hontz, interview with author.

[48]Berger and Luckmann, *Social Construction of Reality*, p. 37.

[49]Ibid., p. 38.

[50]Ibid. This is somewhat in line with Tom Long's understanding that we talk ourselves into being Christian.

We normally found our preachers through divine election—meaning we begged and pleaded until someone agreed to do it. This particular year, however, fifteen-year-old Jake Revere begged to speak. He put down his thoughts on paper and met me in my office to share his words. His opening line was, "I'm going to encourage the congregation to try to give God 80 percent of their lives."

Given my own understanding that discipleship involves the dedication of one's entire life, I found his words quite interesting. "Tell me more, Jake," I prompted.

"Well," he said, "I've got a pretty good handle on most of my life. My friends, my family. But there are those areas that I think would be better if I just gave them over to God. My future is something I don't really have a handle on, so that's something I want to give to God. I just think it would be really great if the congregation could give 80 percent of their lives to God."

I agreed with Jake that, indeed, a congregation that was 80 percent committed to the Lord would be a great thing. I then asked Jake to describe to me how he viewed God.

"He's loving," Jake said, "and he's perfect. And he wants good things for me."

Next I took a piece of paper, ripped it in ten pieces and asked Jake to write down ten different areas of his life that were important to him. These small bits of paper were soon labeled with things like family, friends, schoolwork, theater, youth group, health, future and so on.

Finally, I asked Jake to identify for me the eight aspects of his life he wanted to give to this perfect God as well as the two aspects he wanted to hold on to himself.

There was a long moment of silence before Jake made a comment that has stuck with me all these years: "I see where you're going with this, Pastor Amanda. Why give God 80 percent if I can give him 100?"[51]

Jake came into my office with a preciously unstated theological understanding of God. By articulating this understanding and holding it at arm's length, Jake was able to examine it in ways he might not have been

---

[51]Less than a year after delivering this message to his congregation, Jake Revere was killed in a skiing accident on March 7, 2008. Jake's life and words continue to minister to all who were blessed to know him.

able to had it simply remained unstated in his head. My job was not necessarily to correct Jake's thinking; rather, my role was to reflect back his spoken words and pose questions to him that would allow him to explore his developing thought.

Even the *attempt* to articulate may shed light on our beliefs. A friend of mine shared a testimony concerning a recent experience with doubt. His wife and infant son were away for the week and Jarod was home alone. During this week's time, doubts concerning his faith began to creep into his mind. These doubts grew exponentially as his solitary week went on.

He was both eager and anxious to share his doubt with his wife upon her return. When he sat down and opened his mouth to speak, however, he found he couldn't utter a word. The doubts that had been so large and oppressive while dormant in his mind seemed silly and insignificant when he tried to voice them. "I couldn't even say them," he said. The minute he tried to articulate these particular doubts, he realized there was no power in those fears and felt those particular doubts dissipate. Sometimes simply saying something out loud (or in this case, *almost* saying something out loud) changes our perspective.[52]

> **Often we do not know what we think until we say it. And then, once the words have been spoken, we have a draft from which we can tweak or edit our opinions and beliefs.**

Good writers will tell you that often they have to write multiple drafts until they come to the final product. This kind of drafting is just as crucial with the spoken words. Often we do not know what we think until we say it. And then, once the words have been spoken, we have a draft from which we can tweak or edit our opinions and beliefs.

Seventeen-year-old Abby shared with me the benefits of articulating an experience with God to a peer: "It makes it so much more real to me. When I have an experience with God, it's him and I [*sic*]. Bringing in another person that I can talk about it with makes the experience even more impacting."[53] Dana shares something similar. She explains that

---

[52]Jarod Osborne, interview by Amanda Drury, written record, College Wesleyan Church, Marion, Indiana, October 1, 2013.

[53]Abby X, interview by Amanda Drury, written record, Spring Lake, Michigan, December 18, 2008.

while talking about God to her peers makes her feel uncomfortable, there are benefits: you are "outside your comfort zone because you actually have to look at your life from a different perspective."[54] These two teenagers recognize that articulating their experiences with God somehow deepens their understanding of that experience.

Implicit in the above argument is that this kind of articulation takes place in a conversation with another person. Berger and Luckmann deem conversation the "most important vehicle of reality-maintenance."[55] It is not enough to sit in an empty room by oneself and speak aloud; there is something that takes place within a conversation with another individual that privileges a kind of reality. So we might pose the question akin to the adage of the tree falling in the woods: if a testimony is given without an audience to hear is it still a testimony? I argue it is not. Testifying requires reception.

Of course, Berger and Luckmann admit, this stress on conversation "does not deny the rich aura of non-verbal communication that surrounds speech. Nevertheless speech retains a privileged position to the total conversation apparatus."[56] "Reality-maintenance" within conversation is implicit, not explicit; "Most conversation does not . . . define the nature of the world. Rather, it takes place against the background of a world that is silently taken for granted."[57] Conversation implicitly maintains the reality of how one perceives the world.

Not only does conversation help maintain an ongoing reality, Berger and Luckmann explain that it also "modifies it. Items are dropped and added, weakening some sectors of what is still being taken for granted and reinforcing others. *Thus the subjective reality of something that is never talked about comes to be shaky.*"[58] According to Berger and Luckmann, for better or worse, "Conversation gives firm contours to items previously apprehended in a fleeting and unclear manner." This is true in both affirming one's faith as well as doubting one's faith. "One may have doubts about one's religion," Berger and Luckmann explain, but "these doubts

---

[54]Dana X, interview by Amanda Drury, written record, Marion, Indiana, December 19, 2008.
[55]Berger and Luckmann, *Social Construction of Reality*, p. 152.
[56]Ibid.
[57]Ibid.
[58]Ibid., p. 153, emphasis mine.

become real in a quite different way as one discusses them. One then 'talks oneself into' these doubts [and] they are objectified as reality within one's own consciousness."[59] The doubts one might entertain in one's mind take a firmer shape and contour as they are voiced for both the listener and the speaker to consider as subjective reality.

Maintaining this kind of subjective reality requires our conversations to be continual and consistent. At the same time, Berger and Luckmann explain that occasionally a lack of frequency can be compensated for by the intensity of the conversation that takes place. This explains why a teenager might pick up on more religious language and imagery in a week away at church camp as opposed to one hour's worth of exposure once a week for the entire year at church. Berger and Luckmann give these short but intense conversations "privileged status" and claim they are often found in conversations held with one's confessor, psychoanalyst, or "authority" figure.[60]

In sum, through conversation, our own subjectivities become available to us. For better or worse, the conversations we participate in maintain and modify how we perceive the world. Through articulation we find firmer contours to what we believe (and do not believe) and how we perceive reality. These conversations are most effective when they are constant and continual with the exception of those conversations that hold a certain intensity or privileged status.

Not only does conversation maintain and modify reality (again, *reality* used in the weak sense of the term), it also allows the listener to experience what is being described in a vicarious kind of way. Though I have not walked through the sand in the Sahara Desert, it can be described to me in such a way that I feel as if I have been there. Berger and Luckmann give the example of an individual describing the experience of hunting to young men who have not yet had this experience. "As this experience is designated and transmitted linguistically," they write, "it becomes accessible and, perhaps, strongly relevant to individuals who have never gone through it."[61]

---

[59] Ibid.
[60] Ibid., p. 154.
[61] Ibid., p. 68.

Translated to the church, I may not have seen the Lord provide for me in the way God has provided for my friend, but when I hear this friend testify to God's provisions, I am given insight into the character of God refracted through my friend's experience. I can have vicarious faith that affects my understanding of my own relationship with God.

In the interviews I conducted, this kind of vicarious faith seemed to be stronger when teenagers heard testimonies from their peers. Abby explained: "Hearing a testimony from someone my age opens my eyes to the way my amazing God can use anyone of any age to do his work."[62]

"I seem to relate to a testimony from my own age better," said Krista. "It's easier to understand and comprehend their reactions and feelings."[63]

I may not have seen the Lord provide for me in the way God has provided for my friend, but when I hear this friend testify to God's provisions, I am given insight into the character of God refracted through my friend's experience. I can have vicarious faith that affects my understanding of my own relationship with God.

Sophie echoed Abby's and Krista's thoughts: "It's really cool to see how God is working in the lives of teens, especially my age. I can almost relate to them more."[64]

Hannah explained that she tends to "listen more" if the speaker is her age, though she does not know why.[65] There is something about hearing about the experiences of people their own age that exposes teenagers to the possibility of vicarious faith.

Youth pastors confirm this attentiveness to peer-on-peer testifying. Pastor David Kujawa regularly provides his teenagers opportunities to speak about their relationships with God. When a teenager steps on stage, he says, "you can hear a pin drop." He jokes that there is something "magical" that occurs when a teenager is speaking as opposed to an adult: "Unless the adult has earned a place of leadership and men-

---

[62] Abby X interview.

[63] Krista X, interview by Amanda Drury, written record, Marion, Indiana, December 2008.

[64] Sophie X, interview by Amanda Drury, written record, Holland, Michigan, December 2008.

[65] "Well if there [sic] preaching I can relate to what there [sic] going through, and I do tend to listen more if there [sic] my age, I don't know why." Hannah X, interview by Amanda Drury, written record, Holland, Michigan, December 2008.

torship in that student's mind . . . [their words] probably [don't] apply.
. . . When they hear one of their *peers* speaking . . . it's challenging them
to go further."[66]

Youth pastor Jayson Brewer explains:

> What I say week in and week out can sometimes not hold as much weight as
> the student who testifies to, "This is what God is doing and I'm in the same
> school as you. I'm dealing with the same things as you. And, this is what God
> is saying to me—what God is bringing me through. I have the same struggles
> as you." That testimony, once it's shared, can help someone else who is strug-
> gling with the same thing.[67]

These teenagers, he goes on to explain,

> are very used to being preached at. And it's not just the preachers; it's teachers,
> parents saying: "This is what you need to do," or "This is how you need to live."
> . . . And so, sometimes to the teenagers I'm just another adult. And so when
> they hear from a *student* that they look up to . . . they go, "Whoa, that's right
> where I'm at." . . . They tend to connect with the other teenager and think,
> "Maybe I'll try this God thing out. Maybe it will work for me." . . . And so I try
> to empower them to empower their friends, to empower other people.[68]

Youth pastor and professor Charlie Alcock also speaks of the ea-
gerness of teenagers to hear from their own peers. He tells the story
of booking the well-recognized rock band Switchfoot to play at a
youth event in San Diego. As far as attendance was concerned, the
youth group had just as many teenagers attend a concert given by two
local high school bands as attended the concert for the nationally
known Switchfoot. "They want to see themselves," Alcock explains.
"They want to hear their friends."[69] This realization was one among
many that prompted Charlie to make space for regular testifying
among his teenagers.[70]

---

[66]David Kujawa, interview by Amanda Drury, digital recording, Central Wesleyan Church, Holland, Michigan, December 2, 2008.

[67]Jayson Brewer, interview by Amanda Drury, digital recording, Daybreak Community Church,
Hudsonville, Michigan, June 2, 2009.

[68]Ibid.

[69]Charlie Alcock, interview by Amanda Drury, digital recording, College Wesleyan Church,
Marion, Indiana, June 7, 2009.

[70]I will go into greater depth about what this looks like in the final chapter.

Language allows me to speak about events I am not directly facing, "including some matters I never have and never will experience directly." According to Berger and Luckmann, this allows for language to become, "the objective repository of vast accumulations of meaning and experience, which . . . can then preserve in time and transmit to following generations."[71] There are "spatial, temporal and social dimensions" that are transcended by language.[72] This means language has the ability to "make present those who are currently absent, from the past, or the imagined future."[73] In other words, not only can my faith be strengthened vicariously by those who testify now, I can also draw strength from the testimonies of the cloud of witnesses as recorded in Scripture.

Consequently, there are sociological ramifications with this understanding of language. Simply put, whom we converse with will affect how we understand ourselves. Within "conversation with the new significant others subjective reality is transformed. It is maintained by continuing conversation with them, or within the community they represent."[74] This perhaps explains the stronger likelihood of religious articulacy among evangelical teenagers, as various strands of research have shown the likelihood of strong subcultural forces at work in evangelical settings.[75]

Articulation increases plausibility. Stout reminds us that the language needed to justify one's life-defining commitments is not found in a philosophical framework, but is often embedded within the stories we tell as well as the implicit evaluative frameworks these stories hold.

Stories matter. The narratives we tell have a direct connection with our identities. In "A Short Apology of Narrative," Johann Baptist Metz recounts a story told by Martin Buber in an introduction to Hassidic stories:

> A rabbi, whose grandfather has been a pupil of Baal Shem Tov, was once asked to tell a story. "A story ought to be told," he said, "so that it is itself a help," and his story was this: "My grandfather was paralyzed. Once he was asked to tell a story about a teacher and he told how the holy Baal Shem Tov used to jump

---

[71]Berger and Luckmann, *Social Construction of Reality*, p. 37.

[72]Ibid., p. 39.

[73]Ibid., p. 40.

[74]Ibid., p. 159.

[75]Christian Smith and Michael Emerson, *American Evangelicalism: Embattled and Thriving* (Chicago: University of Chicago Press, 1998).

and dance when he was praying. My grandfather stood up while he was telling the story and the story carried him away so much that he had to jump and dance to show how the master had done it. From that moment, he was healed. This is how stories ought to be told."[76]

When we testify, we articulate the stories that help define who we are. These stories are indelibly linked to our identity.

---

[76]Johann Baptist Metz, "A Short Apology of Narrative," in *Why Narrative?* ed. Stanley Hauerwas and L. Gregory Jones (Grand Rapids: Eerdmans, 1989), p. 253.

What We Say Is Who We Are

Articulating Identity Through Narrative

My declaration of love for my future husband back in 2001 was not only a statement describing my affection for our past relationship; it had huge ramifications for our present and future relationship. Though my statement was made based on past experiences, it was future oriented. Likewise, when we testify, we are not just describing an event that occurred in the past. Our testimony actually helps construct who we are today. A testimony of the past constructs the present and influences the future. When we testify, we articulate the stories that help define who we are. When we are unable to articulate these stories, our identity is threatened. This chapter will address the link between narrative and identity in three different ways. First, we will explore the individual who articulates a life narrative in a meaningful way within time. Second, we will see how the individual's narrative is constructed, maintained and strengthened by the community. Finally, we will see how the relationship between the individual and community serves to uphold a kind of articulate truth telling that we see in everyday life.

Articulating a Life in Time: Personal Narrative, Identity and Testimony

Narrative and identity are indelibly linked. Pastor Jeff Brady learned this the hard way when an accident resulted in complete memory loss. Around 2 a.m. on July 6, 2008, Jeff awoke to an intruder in his house. His wife, Heather, was working the graveyard shift as a nurse in an intensive

care unit. His twelve-year-old stepdaughter was spending the night at
her father's house. His two-year-old son was asleep in his bed. Jeff gives
a detailed description of this event:

> In the middle of the night I heard something stirring around and got up to
> investigate and heard what I thought were burglars downstairs. . . . I grabbed
> my stepdaughter's softball bat right out of the door . . . and chased [an in-
> truder] out of the house. . . . There were at least two [men]. . . . There was one
> right on the back patio by our pool. I must have hit him with the bat because
> everything that he was carrying, our computers and the church laptop that I
> had at home at the time, all that stuff fell into the pool.[1]

Jeff describes the approach of a second burglar and how the two in-
truders knocked him to the ground. He is unsure if he was hit on the
head with the baseball bat or if his head was smashed against the concrete, but Jeff suffered massive blunt-force trauma to his head and passed
out. No one is exactly sure how long Jeff was unconscious, but at some
point he regained consciousness and called for help. When the local law
enforcement arrived, Jeff was still lying on the ground. He was placed on
a stretcher in an ambulance where he relayed the story of the break-in
to the police. He was then rushed to the hospital where he was given a
CT scan of his brain. The scan came back "clean," meaning there was no
visible brain trauma—no bleeding or bruising of any kind. Jeff was able
to follow the doctor's instructions to "follow my finger" and could answer
questions concerning his identity and surroundings. He easily passed all
of the neurological tests presented.[2] Heather, Jeff's wife, was there to pick
him up and drive him home, where the couple promptly went to sleep.
Tragedy averted, the Brady family thought.

Jeff can articulate the story of his accident because it has been *told* to
him. Today he has no memory of this incident. Actually, Jeff has no
memory of anything prior to the accident. He was conscious when the
ambulance came. He was conscious when the CT scans came back "clean."
He was conscious when his wife took him home to rest in the early hours
of the morning. Following the accident, Jeff went to sleep fully aware of

---

[1]Jeff Brady, interview by Amanda Drury, digital recording, Indiana Wesleyan University, Marion,
Indiana, April 2, 2011.
[2]Ibid.

his identity and his surroundings. However, at some point while Jeff slept, memories were erased from his brain.

Jeff awoke around 1 p.m., roughly eleven hours after the accident. He opened his eyes and did not recognize the woman in bed next to him. Jeff recounts this experience:

> I wake up beside [Heather] and at this point in time my brain tells me that I am eighteen years old, that it is . . . Monday, May 16, 2004. I knew it was an exact date for some reason. And I could perfectly recount . . . that just two nights ago I had gone to Buffalo Wild Wings and the go-kart track in Kokomo [Indiana] with my best friend and my older brother. So I wake up and there's this girl beside me, and at that point, when I was eighteen [years old], my parents had been through divorce, a rather nasty one. . . . So I wake up with all these facts swirling in my head and I see this woman beside me that I've never met before and my first thought is, "I had a really cool night or I'm in deep trouble." . . . And I ask Heather . . . "Who are you?" And she says, "You don't remember?" I said, "What do you mean I don't remember?" She said, "You don't know who I am?" And so she tells me she's my wife. I say, "That's crazy. I'm just a senior in high school, I'm about to graduate this Friday, I'm not married or anything," and so with her ICU nurse professionalism . . . she doesn't break down or start crying; she says, "All right we have to go back to the hospital." "Why are we going to the hospital? I'm fine." "No, last night there was a break-in at our house, you had trauma—got hit in the head on the concrete with a baseball bat. We're going to go back to the hospital and get more scans because you should be remembering."[3]

Convinced the woman in bed next to him was crazy, Jeff insisted on seeing his mother, who he thought would set everyone straight.

> We [went] downstairs and there's my mom. She's with the guy who . . . in 2008 was my stepdad, but when I was thinking it was 2004 he was not my stepdad. In fact, I had not met him yet. So here's my mom with this guy who she's saying is her husband and this woman saying she's . . . my wife and I'm her husband. . . . And so [I say], "Fine we'll go to the hospital. They'll get this straightened out. They'll show you guys."[4]

They returned to the hospital where Jeff received more "clean" CT

---

[3]Ibid.
[4]Ibid.

scans. While there was no physical evidence of trauma to the brain, it was clear Jeff's memory was compromised. Jeff was released from the hospital that evening without a diagnosis or a memory. They returned home in an awkward silence, Jeff convinced those around him were crazy.

It was a television commercial that convinced Jeff that perhaps he was the one with the problem—not the people surrounding him.

> [A]s we're watching some TV together . . . a commercial comes on for the Xbox 360 and . . . this is my first thing that's telling me maybe I'm not the one that's right. Because at [age] eighteen, that [Xbox 360] was not out yet; it was not even rumored technology yet. . . . And so now I'm like okay this is weird. . . . They can tell me [made-up] stuff but I know they can't control the programming on TV. So that's kind of the first like, "Something weird is going on."

As traumatic as it was to revert back to his eighteen-year-old self, something much more sinister was brewing in Jeff's brain while he slept. Twenty-four hours after the accident, Jeff awoke on Monday, July 7, and his entire memory was gone. When Jeff awoke, he was no longer his eighteen-year-old self; he was not any kind of "self" at all. Jeff awoke with absolutely no memory of who he was, where he was or even how to function as a normal human being. The woman sleeping next to him told him she was his wife, but Jeff no longer knew what the word *wife* meant. Not only were memories gone, his understanding of relationships and many other concepts was completely lost.

Jeff recalls watching his wife bake cookies in the kitchen soon after the accident. He observed the ding of the oven timer and the emerging cookies. Heather was out of the room when the second batch was finished. She heard the timer, walked into the kitchen and managed to stop Jeff from pulling out the hot cookie sheet with his bare hands. Even the most basic bodily functions were lost on him. When the sensation to defecate emerged he panicked, unsure of what was going on in his own body. "I had no more reference for anything—for social constructs, for social rules, for anything," Jeff explains. "I was at level zero."[5]

Today, roughly eight years later, Jeff has not regained a single memory prior to the accident. He has, however, resumed his duties as a full-time

---

[5]Ibid.

pastor, full-time husband and full-time father. He has enrolled in a master of divinity program to relearn what he had lost in terms of a theological education.[6] While Jeff did not regain his memory, he is once again able to function in society thanks to patient loved ones who retold his stories to him and walked him through life. Without these stories, Jeff was lost.

Life as we know it depends on stories. We are storied people. Stories teach us how to function in society. Alasdair MacIntyre explains that we *become* essentially story-telling animals through our history. We are these story-telling animals through our "actions and practice" as well as in our fictions.[7]

To be a part of human society, MacIntyre explains, is to enter in with "one or more imputed characters—roles into which we have been drafted—and we have to learn what they are in order to be able to understand how others respond to us and how our responses to them are apt to be construed."[8] It is by *hearing* stories that we learn how to act in, construct and interpret our own stories. MacIntyre illustrates this concept:

> It is through hearing stories about wicked stepmothers, lost children, good but misguided kings, wolves that suckle twin boys, youngest sons who receive no inheritance but must make their own way in the world and eldest sons who waste their inheritance on riotous living and go into exile to live with the swine, that children learn or mislearn both what a child and what a parent is, what the cast of characters may be in the drama into which they have been born and what the ways of the world are.[9]

---

[6]Jeff was given the term "muscle memory" to describe how rapidly lost skills returned to him. For example, he found that his fingers could type words on a keyboard almost on their own. He recounts an instance soon after the accident where his fingers absentmindedly skittered across the keyboard leaving sentences he could not decipher: "I would type words I didn't even know what they meant. Like big words like, 'compassionate.' I wrote something about the compassion and care that I'd been receiving and all the loving people who were graciously giving us all these meals and stuff, and [Heather] read it back to me and she said, 'What does that word mean?' 'I don't know.' 'Well you typed it,' [she pushed]. 'I don't know what it means though.' So in the moment of typing it somehow the context of it or something, it made sense to type it, almost like the words weren't my own. I could type this stuff [but] to read it back, it was almost like someone else wrote it. I didn't even know what I was reading, like, 'I wrote that? I don't know those words though.'" Ibid.

[7]Alasdair MacIntyre, *After Virtue: A Study in Moral Theory* (Notre Dame, IN: University of Notre Dame Press, 1984), p. 216.

[8]Ibid.

[9]Ibid.

To put this more concretely, Jeff was missing personal and societal narratives of what married life looked like. He had no reference point. He had no knowledge of what marriage looked like in his family of origin; he did not have a single memory of how Hollywood portrayed the marriage relationship in movies. The idea of marriage was completely foreign to him. It was by hearing stories of his courtship and marriage to Heather that Jeff began to grasp the significance of the marital bond that existed between the two of them. Recognizing the devastation of lacking a narrative, Jeff began to see a therapist simply to train him in what it meant to be a husband.

Stories help us orient ourselves in society. They help us understand who we are and how we relate to society. Without stories, we might echo Jeff's sentiment of feeling as if we are going through "life [as a] walking vegetable."[10]

> Stories help us orient ourselves in society. They help us understand who we are and how we relate to society.

Anthony Rudd explains why narrative is so crucial to our thinking about personal identity. In order to get a clear picture we must understand three concepts and how they relate to one another: (1) narrative, (2) personal identity and (3) time. The three are related and build on one another. Rudd points us in the direction of Ricoeur, who writes of the dependency between time and narrative: "Time becomes human time to the extent it is organized after the manner of narrative; narrative in turn is meaningful to the extent it portrays the features of temporal existence."[11] One's expressed narrative is rooted in time. My personal story is "an act of the imagination that is a patterned integration of [my] remembered past, perceived present, and anticipated future."[12] Operating under the influence of MacIntyre and Charles Taylor, Rudd explains that what is "crucial about narrative is that it links episodes over time in such a way as to make sense of them."[13] Rudd continues:

---

[10]Jeff Brady interview.

[11]Paul Ricoeur, *Time and Narrative*, vol. 1, trans. Kathleen McLaughlin and David Pellauer (Chicago: University of Chicago Press, 1984), p. 52.

[12]Daniel P. McAdams, *The Stories We Live By: Personal Myths and the Making of the Self* (New York: W. Morrow, 1993), p. 12.

[13]Anthony Rudd, "In Defense of Narrative," *European Journal of Philosophy* 17, no. 1 (2007): 61.

Narrative is crucial for the understanding of the identity of persons because narrative (as distinct from chronicle or mere causal sequence) simply is the form in which self-conscious agents make themselves intelligible to themselves as agents persisting through time and therefore through change.[14]

Rudd claims there are three fundamental truths linking narrative, personal identity and time. First, he recognizes that a person is a temporal being—"one whose identity must be a continuing identity through time—unlike, say, the timeless identity of a number."[15] Second, a person possesses self-consciousness. Rudd uses Locke to explain "a being that is able to 'consider itself as itself.'" We are not "a temporally enduring substance such as a rock, or even a tree. A person's persistence through time involves that person's ability to think of him or her self as persisting through time."[16] Third, Rudd explains, "a person is an agent; not just a node in a causal sequence, but a being that acts for reasons."[17]

> **Something integral to one's perceived identity is at stake when that person is unable to articulate his past in a narrative fashion.**

The above assertions are begging for an objection: what about those who are unable to articulate a story? Do they not have identities as well? Are not they people too? Was not Jeff Brady still a human being prior to relearning his story? What of those with Alzheimer's, brain damage or simply the slight memory loss that may come with old age? What of those who neither speak nor have the capacity to remember their narratives? My argument is not that those dealing with the aforementioned conditions are not human—such an assertion is deplorable. I am asserting, however, that when an individual is unable to access his own story, difficulties emerge in his understanding of his self-identity as well as how he fits in with society. Something integral to one's perceived identity is at stake when that person is unable to articulate his past in a narrative fashion.

Everyone has a story whether or not they are able to articulate that story. The eighty-year-old woman with Alzheimer's has a coherent nar-

---

[14]Ibid., p. 63.
[15]Ibid., p. 61.
[16]Ibid.
[17]Ibid.

rative—just one she may no longer have access to. The child born with permanent brain damage lives his story every day—though he may be unable to articulate his lived-out story. When Jeff Brady's memories were erased, it did not change the fact that he nevertheless lived out a coherent story. My point is not that someone is sub-human when he is unable to access his story; rather, a loss of story, or inability to grasp one's story, is a disorienting jolt to one's identity.

Also disorienting is the inability to construct meaning or cohesion within one's story. MacIntyre directs our attention to an individual who attempts suicide. That person might complain "that his or her life is meaningless." Statements of this sort often reveal "that the narrative of their life has become unintelligible to them, that it lacks any point, any movement towards a climax or a *telos*."[18] *Something is lost when we are unable to grasp our own narratives in any kind of meaningful way.*

Originally when I heard Jeff's story of losing his memory I assumed it was a terrifying, disorienting experience. When I shared this assumption with Jeff, he told me otherwise:

> Well, at the time you don't really miss what you don't know you don't have, you know what I mean? So I didn't really know that I was missing anything. I mean I knew that I didn't have my memory but can you really comprehend the lack of an identity until you have one again? . . . I couldn't know what I was missing until I personally experienced it and realized I was missing a lot.[19]

The idea of disruption resulting from the inability to articulate or find significance in one's narrative has been widely accepted among psychologists.[20] I think we can push this further: *just as the inability to recall or find significance in our psychological narrative can be disruptive to our identity, so too can disruption incur if we are unable to recall or find significance in our spiritual narrative.* Just as Jeff was unaware of what he was missing when his memory was at its worst, so too those unable to articulate or find significance in their spiritual stories may not be aware of the disruption to identity that exists. In other words, they simply do not know what they

---

[18]MacIntyre, *After Virtue*, p. 217.
[19]Brady interview.
[20]Oliver Sacks has spoken widely to this effect. Oliver W. Sacks, *The Man Who Mistook His Wife for a Hat and Other Clinical Tales* (New York: Summit Books, 1985).

are missing. If people are not actively articulating their narrative understanding of their faith journeys they risk a disruption similar to a person with amnesia. Regardless of how often a teenager attends her church, if she is unable to articulate some kind of narrative concerning where God is present in her life, she risks upheaval of her spiritual identity.

This is asking a lot, some might say. How can we expect a teenager to speak about something so infinite and transcendent? I should add that by "articulate" I do not mean a kind of precise, poignant speech; rather, I am referring to a verbal acknowledgment that may at times be no more than verbal gesturing, like we see in the man born blind in John 9. When asked who healed him, he responds by simply telling them step by step the narrative of the healing events: "The man they call Jesus made some mud and put it on my eyes. He told me to go to Siloam and wash. So I went and washed, and then I could see" (Jn 9:11). When asked if Jesus was a sinner, the man responds, "Whether he is a sinner or not, I don't know. One thing I do know. I was blind but now I see" (Jn 9:25). The man has little knowledge of what happened or why it happened. He simply speaks to that which he does know: he was blind and now he can see. This is far from an astute, theological treatise. He is simply gesturing toward his own narrative. Following this testimony, the man is confronted once more with Jesus, who fills in some of the gaps of his narrative. The man grows in his understanding of his own narrative through interaction with his community and the passing of time.

Everyone has a spiritual story. Everyone has some kind of narrative that describes his or her spiritual journey. However, not everyone has *access* to this narrative, and even if a person is aware of this narrative, he or she might choose to not articulate it. Regardless of whether or not it is acknowledged or articulated, however, they still have some kind of spiritual narrative. Articulation allows us to bring a story to expression, which is central to constructing identity.

All of this, of course, is based on a theological assertion that God is active and present within the world and interacts with people, and also that we are able to see and identify part of this work. God's transcendence does not limit God to solely being outside the material world. We also account for God's immanence in God's ongoing involvement within the material world.

The fullest expression of Christian living is found in the acknowledgment and articulation of where a person sees Jesus Christ at work in his or her life. This assertion is not meant to challenge the notion of an "anonymous Christian"[21] nor downplay the significance of apophatic theology. Rather, I am acknowledging the formative effect an acknowledged and articulated faith might have on an individual. This may sound like a big task to some, particularly when it comes to talking about God. The kind of relationship with God that I am holding up as the standard is one where an individual seeks to acknowledge and articulate where God is at work in his life.

> **The fullest expression of Christian living is found in the acknowledgment and articulation of where a person sees Jesus Christ at work in his or her life.**

This is difficult enough for adults to do, never mind teenagers. Nevertheless, this daunting call for spiritual articulation is well suited for teenagers. Clinical psychologist Daniel McAdams speaks of adolescence as heralding "the beginning of mythmaking proper in the human life cycle, as teenagers begin to see their lives in storied, historical terms."[22] McAdams speaks of adolescence as bringing with it "the development of formal thought and the emergence of a historical perspective on the self."[23] Early adolescence ushers in a new era in which teenagers begin to think of their life as an unfolding narrative in which they hold some kind of agency. In other words, during adolescence teenagers are actively constructing their identity. That is not to say they are constructing their identity out of nothing; rather, they have been "'collecting material' for [their] story since Day One, even though [they do not] remember Day One."[24] The concept of a story is acquired early in life. According to psychologist Theodore Sarbin, the main difference between a young child's story and an adult's story is what is emphasized. Young children tend to emphasize "melodic patterns" and tend not to transition

---

[21]Karl Rahner, *A Rahner Reader,* ed. Gerald A. McCool (New York: Seabury Press, 1975), pp. 214, 220.

[22]McAdams, *Stories We Live By*, p. 13.

[23]Ibid., p. 277.

[24]Ibid., p. 40.

to more plot-oriented stories until they are around ten years of age.[25] So while children are able to grasp the concept of their story, it is often not until the adolescent years that they are able to search for a plot and meaning within that story.[26] While acknowledging and articulating where God might be active may sound like a daunting task, the teenager is not working alone. The teenager's community is needed. In fact, true testimony *requires* a community. A testimony requires an audience to exist in its fullness.[27] You cannot have a testimony without a community.

ARTICULATED SELF: COMMUNITY IN THE CONSTRUCTION, MAINTENANCE AND STRENGTHENING OF A PERSONAL NARRATIVE IDENTITY

On the morning of August 31, 2004, employees of a Burger King in Richmond Hill, Georgia, found a man unconscious next to a dumpster. "He was naked, he had bug bites from red ants, he appeared to be beaten," said special agent Bill Kirkconnell of the FBI. He also had amnesia and was unable to remember his own name, much less how he came to be found beaten behind a Burger King. The man was ultimately diagnosed with organic retrograde amnesia due to trauma to the head.[28]

---

[25]Theodore R. Sarbin, *Narrative Psychology: The Storied Nature of Human Conduct* (New York: Praeger, 1986), p. xii.

[26]One might understand this identity construction through the lens of subject-object relations. Educational theorist Robert Kegan identifies a pivotal shift that occurs in adolescence in *In Over Our Heads: The Mental Demands of Modern Life* (Cambridge, MA: Harvard University Press, 1994). In the transition from childhood to adolescence, the ordering of and relationships between what is subject and object undergo a transformation. Within subject-object relations, Kegan explains, "'Object' refers to those elements of our knowing or organizing that we can reflect on, handle, look at, be responsible for, relate to each other, take control of, internalize, assimilate, or otherwise operate upon. . . . It is distinct enough from us that we can do something with it" (p. 32). This is contrasted with "subject," which "refers to those elements of our knowing or organizing that we are identified with, tied to, fused with, or embedded in." He explains further, "We *have* objects; we *are* subjects. We cannot be responsible for, in control of, or reflect on that which is subject. Subject is immediate; object is mediate. Subject is ultimate or absolute; object is relative" (ibid.). Much of developmental psychology speaks of adolescence as an emerging time when teenagers think about themselves as storied selves with agency.

[27]Words that may be understood as part of a testimony within a community take on a different function when we speak aloud alone. Instead of a testimony we are dealing with praise or confession, depending on the content.

[28]David Lohr, "Meet Benjaman Kyle: The Man with No Identity," AOL News, September 13, 2010, accessed July 16, 2011, at www.aolnews.com/2010/09/13/meet-benjaman-kyle-the-man-with-no-identity.

This man's story is very similar to Jeff Brady's in that both are unable to retrieve stored memories. Jeff's memories begin twenty-four hours after the accident. The memories of the man found behind Burger King begin soon after he awoke in a hospital. There is, however, one large exception to the similarity between the two stories: Jeff had a community; the other man did not. Jeff had a community to tell him his name when he woke up. The other man did not and took on the assumed name Benjaman Kyle. Jeff was surrounded by family and friends to fill in the gaps of his life pre-accident. The other man was not. Jeff had a pastor and a congregation who took months training him back into his profession as a pastor. The other man is unsure of his vocation pre-accident. Jeff's family walked him through everyday functions, slowly introducing him back to society. The other man had no such help and at one point found himself living in a homeless shelter.[29] Today Jeff is a husband, a father, a pastor and a student. Jeff has regained a normal life. If you were to meet Jeff today you would have no idea of the trauma he has endured. The other man is far from socialized into society. He has nowhere near the peace and security Jeff enjoys. "I hate that I don't have a lot of control of my life," the man says. "I have no money, I can't drive [and] I can't get a job. Basically, other people seem to rule my life. I don't have a lot of choice in it, and I hate that."[30] Since he has no way of verifying his given name, he has been unable to secure a Social Security card and can neither obtain a job nor collect any kind of benefits from the government.[31] This man has exhausted his options of seeking out a community that knew him prior to his accident. His story has been featured on various daytime talk shows and evening news programs. But no one has come forth to offer insight into his identity. He has a narrative. He has a story. And no doubt this narrative would shed light on his identity as the two are so indelibly linked. Without a community, however, this man has no access to his story, and today he has a difficult time finding joy and meaning in who he is.

Both men's stories are no doubt more dramatic that what most of us encounter in our everyday lives. However, the extreme nature of their

---

[29]Ibid.
[30]Ibid.
[31]Ibid.

cases highlights for us the powerful and necessary role community plays in our understanding of narrative and personal identity. No one exists in his or her own narrative by him- or herself. Everyone's story holds within it supporting characters. We do not exist within a vacuum. Alasdair MacIntyre explains:

> For the story of my life is always embedded in the story of those communities from which I derive my identity. I am born with a past; and to try to cut myself off from that past, in the individualist mode, is to deform my present relationships. The possession of an historical identity and the possession of a social identity coincide. Notice that rebellion against my identity is always one possible mode of expressing it.[32]

Narrative and identity are indelibly linked. It is not enough, however, to say that an isolated experience shapes one's life; we must also take into account how that event is experienced, understood and recorded as well as how it is shared with others. Here again we see the critical role of the community. My community helps train my eyes to see where God is at work in my life. My community helps supply my mouth with language to narrate these experiences. And my community provides me with a framework in which I might interpret these experiences.

Communities are critical in the interplay between narrative and identity. A community is needed to receive a testimony. There is not a testimony without someone there to receive the testimony. A person talking aloud in a room by herself is not testifying; she is simply talking aloud in a room. Those who hear the testimony are not merely listening devices that impartially take in a testimony. Those who hear the testimony *receive* it. They are pulled into the scene and are a part of the story. One person might be speaking, but the community as a whole receives and participates in this testimony. I want teenagers to testify, but it is just as important to have a community to receive that testimony. While there might be benefits in speaking aloud by oneself in a room (persuasion theory), the benefits greatly increase when the words are shared within a community. These communities that helped give us the eyes to see God at work as well as the language to testify to these experiences also help

---

[32]MacIntyre, *After Virtue*, p. 221.

us construct, interpret and strengthen our spiritual identities.

When I testify, I testify to events I have experienced and interpreted through the lens of my community. Though my experience may have seemed like a personal and private interaction between God and me, my community is always informing this experience. The way that I see myself and the way I understand God's interaction with me are largely shaped by my community. That is not to say that the community *creates* these experiences, only that the lens in which I see and interpret these experiences is tinted by my social context.

Community and the construction of narrative identity. We do not and cannot foster our own spiritual identity by ourselves; communities are what help us *construct* our narrative identities, *maintain* our narrative identities and *strengthen* our narrative identities. Communities also help hold narrative identities to a kind of *accountability*, a topic of special interest in my project since questions are often raised concerning false testimony. Unlike most of us, Jeff Brady was able to see explicit ways in which his community helped construct (or reconstruct) his narrative identity. While every aspect of his life was reconstructed by his community, for the sake of my argument, I will focus my attention on the reconstruction of his spiritual identity. The reconstruction of his spiritual narrative came following Jeff's exposure to works of fiction. Within a week or two of his accident Jeff was able to read on his own.[33] Jeff describes the "great escape" he experienced in reading the fiction on his bookshelf. Around the third week, Heather asked her husband, "When are you going to read something nonfiction?" "That stuff's boring," Jeff

---

[33]Again we see evidence of liquid memory or muscle memory emerge. Many of the skills that Jeff had mastered prior to the accident (such as reading) came back to him quickly with some effort. Speaking of a meeting with his neuropsychologist, Jeff says, "I think our third or fourth session together, he put me through a rigorous IQ test and a lot of it was like math based, or remember these shapes and stuff, and I was killing it on all of it until we got to this trivia bit about the temperature of boiling water or something like that, and I didn't know that factual stuff, and he said, your brain is just so unique, I mean everyone's brains are, but he just couldn't get over it how . . . I was killing it on the shape recognition or even some basic math functions. I couldn't do the higher stuff like, you know, three-digit multiplication in my head, but the simpler stuff I was just killing it and so he told me frequently that every brain's unique and if what happened to me happened to him he might be in a very different situation than me. And so I guess that has been pretty formative to me that what happened to me was unique, it could have happened similarly to someone else, but it could have been very worse [sic], or it could be not as severe." Brady interview.

responded, explaining how fiction helped him escape from his current situation. "Well you don't have to," Heather continued, "but maybe you should try this one." She handed him a Bible.[34]

Jeff explains his initial interaction with the Scriptures:

> I flipped through it, and I read some stuff, but it didn't make a lot of sense and it didn't connect with me. Especially without a lot of guidance.... You just flip open, you hit Numbers and Leviticus, horrible.... The Psalms? They were interesting but I didn't get it. *Who's this "God" that you're singing of?* Matthew, Mark and Luke? There were some interesting stories there, you know, it was almost like Gandalf or something. This guy can turn water into wine and make people walk and stuff? But it didn't connect in the heart; it didn't connect on a spiritual level. I only read a little bit of it here and there, and put it back down and went back to Harry Potter: fun stuff.

Communities are what help us *construct* our narrative identities, *maintain* our narrative identities and *strengthen* our narrative identities.

His desire to reconnect with the faith he held prior to his accident was prompted by the comments made by those around him. "I hope he comes back" was a comment Jeff regularly heard. It bothered him and left him with the impression that he was not "good enough" the way he was.

> [T]hey're all hoping for healing, for me to be restored, but I don't remember that. I'm thinking I am who I am. Obviously, maybe there's something to be desired, but this is my state of mind, this is who I am. After a few weeks that kind of ... bothered me a bit, to the point of, all right, fine, let's figure this out.... I looked at lots of stuff: Islam, Hindu writings, Kabbalah stuff, and some of that stuff's kind of compelling, about peace and prayer and things like that, but none of it resonated. And so after a couple weeks of all this searching and homework, I finally pick up the Bible again. This is probably like week six [after the accident], and I just [said], *All right, I don't know if there's any sort of God out there, but everyone seems to think there is, so if my identity used to be in this God and this is your book, then just show me something so that I know you're actually there, because I've got this horrible mistrust.* So I flip the Bible open to James 1: "Consider it pure joy, my brothers, when you face trials and temptations of any kind, if you know that the testing of your faith, perseverance must finish its course so that you may be mature and not lacking in anything." Wow, I'm going through trials

---

[34]Ibid.

and this is not joyful but something about it compelled me and I ate that book up. And you finish James and right there beside it are the two Peters and the three Johns back there in the back, and Jude: fantastic books for someone who doesn't know anything. First John 4: "This is love: that God gave his Son for you because of this love, now we need to show it to other people. If you say that you love God but not with your brother or sister: liar." Whoa . . . when I started reading the Gospel of John again about the Word and the truth and the life and the Word was with God, something about it came together in that moment in week seven, where I said, "All right, I don't know who you are, but I think you're out there and I now think that you're real, and if that's the case then I accept the fact that you love me and I understand this goal that you have for me to be with you and so I'm going to make the decision now to follow what I've read and try to apply it to my life and I don't know really what all that means in the long run, but I'm going to follow the Bible." That was kind of my new start with faith.[35]

It was also around this time when Jeff's senior pastor, Roger, started emerging once again in his life. He casually asked Jeff questions about what he was reading, "never pushing me toward spiritual things," Jeff explains, simply to carry on conversations. Obviously, Jeff was unable to perform his duties as a youth pastor. While some churches may have been tempted to terminate his position or give him an unpaid leave of absence, Jeff's church community continued to pay his salary and, in fact, encouraged him to spend as much time as he wanted at the church office without any obligations.[36]

So Jeff began going to the church during the week. He did so, however, with a pair of sunglasses on. Sunglasses for Jeff became a safety barrier from the foreign, outside world. He explains: "I felt in that moment as they were looking at me and my eyes they could see more about me than I knew about me. That they knew me better than I knew myself. So from day two or three [after the accident] on for quite a while I wore sunglasses everywhere."[37]

Jeff visited the church throughout the week with his sunglasses on while Roger slowly introduced him to various church staff tasks. He went from stamping envelopes to entering data into computers to eventually partnering with other staff members to prepare spiritual formation lit-

---

[35]Ibid.
[36]Ibid.
[37]Ibid.

erature. Jeff met with Carol, a Sunday school coordinator, to write a Bible study. Carol encouraged Jeff to write the literature based on his own spiritual questions. Jeff explains how this booklet consisted of questions like "Who's God? How do I know that he's really there? If I know God, what does that mean for my life? What are the implications?" What Carol did, Jeff explains, was help "me put my own journey on paper." For the first time Jeff was able to articulate his spiritual narrative post-accident and record it as such. Jeff's spiritual journey and identity were becoming accessible to him in a new way.

The whole congregation came together for Jeff's first Sunday back at church. Pastor Roger had prepared the congregation. Jeff recalls his pastor's guidance to the church community: "I know Jeff used to be a real big hugger with you guys, very personable and everything; you can't be that way with him, he's different now. He's nervous and scared so he's going to come in after the service starts and after the service is over, I'm going to ask you guys to please not rush over to where he'll be sitting, but just go out the way you normally do. Don't make any extra efforts toward him, because he's really scared about coming."

Jeff arrived at church, with his sunglasses on and sat behind the sound booth, attempting to take advantage of a physical barrier between himself and the congregation. Six weeks in, he says, he stood up in front of the congregation to give announcements—still with his sunglasses on, but he was slowly being brought back into the life of the church as well as into a deeper understanding of himself and what it meant to be a child of God.

His visits to the office increased to four times a week, and about five months after the accident, Pastor Roger invited Jeff to resume his duties as a youth pastor. Jeff's wife, Heather, challenged him, "'If you're going to do this, you have to stop wearing the glasses.' And so we tried church one day without the glasses. I really thought it was going to kill me, but it didn't and so we do church without the glasses, and I go to youth group that night and just hang out, not really being the youth pastor, just hanging out. And the next week I actually try a lesson playing a game with them and the kids were very understanding."[38]

---

[38]Ibid.

Jeff's church community played an intensive role in helping him come to know and understand his identity. Jeff cannot help but wonder where his life might have ended up if not for the support of his church community:

> What if I'd gone home with Mom? What if I'd been in a different church? What if I'd been one pastor among twenty in a church of one thousand? What if I'd been a solitary pastor and once that pastor gets knocked out of the church they have to find a new one, and so long Jeff? What if any of it had been different? Would I have recovered the way I did?[39]

Again, while I doubt many of us have had an experience remotely similar to Jeff's, the dramatic nature of his experience gives us an interesting and lucid look at what identity construction within community looks like. Our stories may be vastly different from Jeff's, but the involvement of community as a formative force is just as present in our own stories as it was in Jeff's. We are constructed by community. We are not constructed in isolation. Berger and Luckmann claim that no one can "be adequately understood apart from the particular social context in which they were shaped."[40] Our identities are negotiated through dialogical relationships with others, Taylor explains, "partly overt, partly internalized."[41]

This does not mean that we are simply mirrors of our community. We are shaped by our community and often understood in light of our community, but that does not mean that we look identical to our community. MacIntyre explains that we do not have to accept the moral limitations of our particular community, but without "those moral particularities to begin from there would never be anywhere to begin."[42] A young person rebelling against his community of faith is just as formed by that community as the young person who adheres to its values and faith distinctives. We are shaped by the community that surrounds us. Taylor explains, "It would take a great deal of effort, and probably many wrenching break-ups, to prevent our identity being formed by the people we love. . . . If some of the things I value

---

[39]Ibid.

[40]Berger and Luckmann, *Social Construction of Reality*, p. 50.

[41]Charles Taylor, *The Ethics of Authenticity* (Cambridge, MA: Harvard University Press, 1992), p. 47.

[42]MacIntyre, *After Virtue*, p. 221.

most are accessible to me only in relation to the person I love, then she becomes internal to my identity."[43] We are shaped by our community regardless of whether or not we agree with what the community values.

Communities shape people. We are not the only characters in our personal narratives; our story did not fall into our mind free of others' fingerprints. The stories we share and the ways in which we construct meaning in our life are

> **The stories we share and the ways in which we construct meaning in our life are largely due to the company we keep.**

largely due to the company we keep. The identity construction offered by Jeff's church community shapes how Jeff sees and understands God to be present and active in his life. The way that Jeff speaks about God today is significantly influenced by his church community. Apart from what Jeff says about God, the fact that Jeff is even comfortable speaking of God in everyday conversation is a reflection of the values and emphases given to him by his community. A teenager who grows up in a home or church where there is continual and consistent talk of God's presence has been constructed in such a way as to notice and perhaps even expect God to be present and at work in her life. Again, that is not to say that the community fabricates the presence or activities of God (though that may be the case in some environments), only that the community is teaching its members to *look* for God at work.

Community and the maintenance of narrative identity. Communities not only help construct narrative spiritual identity, they also help *maintain* one's narrative spiritual identity. Chapter two ended with sociological ramifications for operating under an understanding of subjective reality and community. This section takes those notions a bit further.

At the risk of sounding cynical, I imagine many youth pastors from evangelical backgrounds would attest to the frequency of adolescents reporting conversion experiences. Popular guest speakers prompt teenagers to "raise a hand" or "come to the altar," demonstrating their commitment to follow Christ. These experiences are easy, Berger and Luckmann explain. "To have a conversion experience is nothing much. The real thing is to be able to keep on taking it seriously; to retain a sense of its plausibility. This

---

[43]Taylor, *Ethics of Authenticity*, p. 34.

is where religious community comes in. It provides the indispensable plausibility structure for the new reality."[44] Using the apostle Paul as an example, Berger and Luckmann explain how "Saul may have become Paul in the aloneness of religious ecstasy, but he could remain Paul only in the context of the Christian community that recognized him as such and confirmed the 'new being' in which he now located this identity."[45]

This type of narrative spiritual identity maintenance emerges as a kind of spiritual socialization. Berger and Luckmann explain that a Catholic can only *remain* a Catholic through socialization with other Catholics. "Disruption of significant conversation with the mediators of the respective plausibility structures threatens the subjective realities in question."[46] In other words, when the community that props up plausibility structures is absent, we may have difficulty maintaining our beliefs. That is not to say the community is the author of our faith, only that the community is often a conduit of nurturing the Holy Spirit's gift of faith.

Accents of reality are lost, Berger and Luckmann explain, when individuals are isolated from the community to which they identify:

> The individual living for many years among people of a different faith and cut off from the community of those sharing his own may continue to identify himself as, say, a Catholic. Through prayer, religious experiences, and similar techniques his old Catholic reality may continue to be subjectively relevant to him. At the very least the techniques may sustain his continued self-identification as a Catholic. They will, however, become subjectively empty of "living" reality unless they are "revitalized" by social contact with other Catholics. To be sure, an individual usually remembers the realities of his past. But the way to "refresh" these memories is to converse with those who share their relevance.[47]

Berger and Luckmann conclude with an observation: recognizing the role community plays in our understanding of our spiritual identity, "one must . . . be very careful with whom one talks."[48]

---

[44]Berger and Luckmann, *Social Construction of Reality*, p. 158. By "plausibility structure," Berger and Luckmann are referring to those systems or sociocultural contexts that uphold certain beliefs, making them appear to be more plausible.
[45]Ibid.
[46]Ibid., p. 155.
[47]Ibid.
[48]Ibid., p. 159.

This understanding of community helping to maintain identity corresponds with the practice of testimony in at least two ways. First, the maintenance of a community can help affirm what has been testified. So a congregant may remind another congregant of his earlier words, thereby affirming and reinforcing what was testified. Second, while an individual may not have multiple conversion experiences, she may hear testimonies of others' conversion experiences and, in hearing others' stories, may find her own faith buttressed. Similarly, hearing the words of young confirmands may affirm and reinforce one's own experience of confirmation. Often, the baptismal liturgy in high-church liturgies serves as this kind of reminder. This can be particularly meaningful for churches that practice infant baptism. While adults may not remember their own baptism as infants, they can join in on the collective memory of the church and hear the words of identity that were spoken over them. Though we may go through a time when we are not able to sense the presence of God, hearing about others' experiences may help maintain our understanding of our own spiritual narrative vicariously.

Christian Smith points out another key area in which community helps maintain identity. We maintain who we are by acknowledging who we are not. Smith claims that evangelicals draw symbolic boundaries between in and out groups. They come to know who they are largely by knowing who they are not. In other words, "every 'yes' automatically begets a 'no.'"[49]

We see this kind of identify-forming distinction emerge in various kinds of testimonies. Someone may contrast her own actions with what the world would have her do: "The world told me to do X, but I did Y instead." Or, the testifier may offer a contrast between who she used to be and who she is today in a "I-once-was-lost-but-now-am-found" way. Those who are within a particular community are able to better maintain their identity by acknowledging their distinction from those outside of the community.

Community and the strengthening of identity. An articulated narrative has the potential to be strengthened when shared within the community. For example, fifteen-year-old Tyler testifies to his experience of spending his Saturday working at the local soup kitchen. He shares about

---

[49]Smith, *American Evangelicalism*, p. 92.

the hard work, explains what he did in the kitchen, and confesses feelings of discomfort as well as the satisfaction he felt after doing something he believes God wanted him to do. If the community receives this testimony and affirms it in such a way that they help Tyler ascribe value to his efforts, Tyler might be more inclined to work at the soup kitchen again. Or perhaps fourteen-year-old Sarah testifies to feeling called to the ministry. The community receives this testimony, and if they affirm her sense of call, Sarah is strengthened in her desire and call to minister.

What we see emerge is a kind of articulacy loop. Within this loop an individual undergoes some kind of experience that he either believes is from God, or at least questions whether it is from God. Next, the speaker bears witness of this experience to his community in the form of a testimony. The community then offers feedback. This feedback could take one of three forms. First, the community may affirm what has been shared. Second, the community may provide additional information for the speaker to gain greater insight. Third, it could be that the community is critical of the testimony and questions its validity, or the speaker's inter-

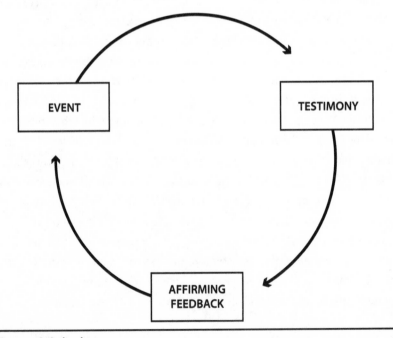

Figure 3.1. Articulacy loop

pretation of the event. Each one of these forms of feedback can strengthen the spiritual identity of the speaker. The first serves as a kind of affirmation. The second seeks to supply greater information to the speaker, thereby clarifying and strengthening his identity. Both of these responses affirm the experience and the testimony of the speaker and may serve as a catalyst for him to continue to seek out the presence of God and testify to what he has experienced. The third, more critical response may be painful for the speaker, but it nevertheless can serve as a spiritually formative corrective. This kind of "articulacy loop" helps train our eyes to look to those places where God might already be at work (see figure 3.1).

I should state that the articulacy loop does not require that you begin with an event. You can enter this loop at any point. Perhaps the community affirms something in you before you testify to its existence.

Not only does the testifier have the opportunity to participate within this cycle, the community is also given the opportunity to participate.

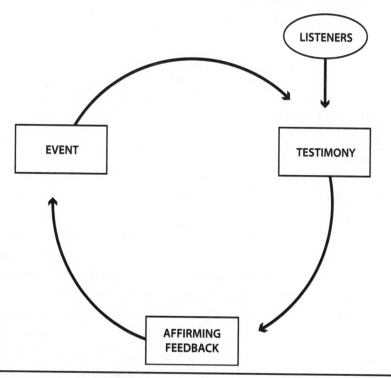

Figure 3.2. Articulacy loop with listeners

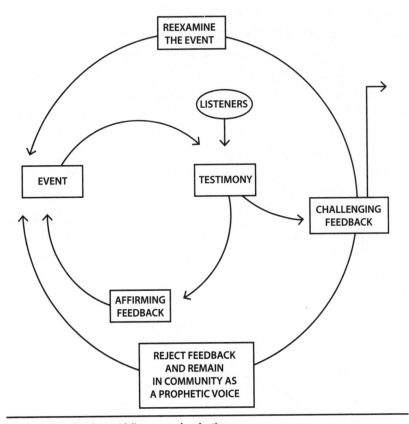

Figure 3.3. Articulacy loop with listeners and evaluation

Josh might hear Tyler's testimony concerning his work at the soup kitchen and decide to participate the following week, which may later prompt a testimony of his own. Jacob might hear Sarah's testimony of feeling called to the ministry and might seek out the community's thoughts on whether or not he too might be called. Every testimony that takes place is an invitation for the rest of the community to participate within the articulacy loop.

Of course, the community's feedback is not always positive. If the community questions the veracity of the testimony, the testifier then has a few options. He can (a) reexamine the original narrative in light of the community's feedback and attempt a new interpretation, (b) simply leave behind the original narrative and attempt to do something new, (c) hold fast to his event and his words of testimony and remain in his community as a medium for prophetic discourse, or (d) leave the community and testify to a new community.[50]

In addition to constructing, maintaining and strengthening narrative identities, communities also serve as a kind of quality control. The community has the responsibility to serve as gatekeepers of a testimony, affirming what they believe is true and questioning or refuting that which does not line up with the community's understanding of God. This challenge to the articulacy loop is a key task within the life of a community as people attempt to articulate truth concerning the presence of Jesus Christ in their lives.

ARTICULATING TRUTH: TESTIMONY IN EVERYDAY LIFE

But what should be done if a testimony is clearly wrong? Perhaps the one who testifies is mistaken in her understanding of her experience? Or worse, what if she is deliberately bearing false witness? Concerns for the preservation of truth have closely followed any practice of testimony. Scripture often states that testimonies would only be accepted in a court of law when there were two or more witnesses.[51] According to Roman law, this number increased to five witnesses where woman and slaves were concerned.

I was a teenager when I heard the testimony of Dr. Anthony Thorpe.[52] Dr. Thorpe was a respected pediatrician in our town and was testifying that God had told him to leave his job and become a medical missionary. We might have applauded and affirmed this call were it not for one thing: Dr. Thorpe also claimed he was to leave his wife and twin boys and marry another woman who would be a more suitable partner for this endeavor. And this is where testimony often gets its negative reputation. How can you discern whether a testimony is true or false? How can you argue with someone who says *God* told him to do something?

We would be wise to remember that a testimony is one's *perceived* rec-

---

[50]Of course, speaking publicly involves risks, and it could be that a person testifying receives challenging feedback and declines to testify in the future. In the final chapter of this book I will address responsible ways of challenging a testimony without discouraging others to share.

[51]"On the testimony of two or three witnesses a person is to be put to death, but no one is to be put to death on the testimony of only one witness" (Deut 17:6). "One witness is not enough to convict anyone accused of any crime or offense they may have committed. A matter must be established by the testimony of two or three witnesses" (Deut 19:15).

[52]Name and minor details have been changed.

ollection of a particular event; it is not the event itself. Again, Ricoeur would remind us that testimony is quasi-empirical, "because testimony is not perception itself but the report, that is, the story, the narration of an event. It consequently transfers things seen to the level of things said."[53]

Borrowing the language and concepts from Berger, Luckmann and Christian Smith discussed in chapter two, we experience Reality and report it as reality. We experience something as it is. Our perception and recollection of this experience, however, are not pure. What we say and do does not create a strong social reality; we are shaped significantly "not only by objective reality but also by . . . social contexts."[54] In some ways you could say that we testify *weakly*. Our testimonies are fraught with social conditioning and personal bias. In other words, there is great margin for error. To testify at all is to open ourselves up to false testimony.

Every time a community hears a testimony they have a choice: should we believe this testimony or should we reject this testimony? C. A. J. Coady presents a consequence matrix that I have whittled into a chart for the sake of convenience to see what is at stake in how we respond to both true and false testimony (see table 3.1).[55]

Table 3.1. Consequence Matrix

	Testimony in reality was true	Testimony in reality was false
Choose to believe the testimony is reliable	Extended true belief with perhaps some false belief	Great extension of error with perhaps some true belief
Choose not to believe testimony is reliable	Great failure to receive available true belief	Great safety from error

Of course, there are testimonies that sound false but are in fact true, potentially resulting in a great failure to receive available truth. John Locke tells a story of the king of Siam declaring a certain Dutch ambassador a liar for claiming that in the Netherlands the water could become so cold and hard an elephant could walk on it. John Locke explains that difficulties arise "when testimonies contradict common experience, and

[53]Ricoeur, *Time and Narrative*, p. 123.
[54]Smith, *What Is a Person?* pp. 121-22.
[55]C. A. J. Coady, *Testimony: A Philosophical Study* (Oxford: Clarendon, 1992).

the reports of history and witnesses clash with the ordinary course of nature, or with one another."[56]

While concerns for the accuracy of testimony can be traced far back through history, it is perhaps within the last century that testifying has been most strongly scrutinized. Harvard psychologist Gordon Allport was at the helm of this scrutiny with his book *The Psychology of Rumor*, where he provided test cases revealing the unreliability of testimonies of eyewitnesses. Subjects were shown a picture of people on a subway train. Train occupants included a white man with a "cutthroat" razor in his hand in an argument with an unarmed black man. After a brief look at the picture, roughly 50 percent of the subjects reported that the razor was held by the black man. Allport concluded that even "neutral" viewers of the picture were incorrect because of latent assumptions concerning race.[57]

More recently the Supreme Court has revisited the reliability of eyewitness testimony in court. Various reports and studies have called into question the reliability of eyewitness testimony, and in the past thirty years research in this area has greatly increased, with "more than 2,000 studies on the topic" being published in various professional journals.[58] In his book *Convicting the Innocent*, Brandon L. Garrett claims that "of the first 250 DNA exonerations, 190 involved eyewitnesses who were wrong."[59]

In 2008 Geoffrey Gaulkin was appointed as a special master by the New Jersey Supreme Court to explore this issue of the reliability of eyewitness testimony. In his report, Gaulkin claims:

---

[56]John Locke, *An Essay Concerning Human Understanding* (New York: Dover Publications, 1959), p. 309. Coady, an Australian philosopher who deals with epistemological problems that emerge in testifying, explains how the works of Locke and Descartes led to a decline in the esteem of testimony to the extent that modern epistemologies tend to neglect testimony, citing it as inferior to other forms of knowledge. Coady, *Testimony*, pp. 13-14.

[57]Gordon Allport and Leo Postman, *The Psychology of Rumor* (New York: Russell & Russell, 1965), pp. 61-74, 87-89, 104, 111.

[58]The last time this subject matter was explored by the Supreme Court was back in 1977. See Adam Liptak, "34 Years Later, Supreme Court Will Revisit Eyewitness IDs," *The New York Times*, August 22, 2011, www.nytimes.com/2011/08/23/us/23bar.html.

[59]Ibid. Today forensic psychologists are often called upon to testify on behalf of defendants to make various cases for the unreliability of eyewitness testimony. See Glenn Fowler, "Robert Buckhout, Writer and Professor of Psychology, 55," *The New York Times*, December 12, 1990, www.nytimes .com/1990/12/12/obituaries/robert-buckhout-writer-and-professor-of-psychology-55.html.

Because the reliability of any reported "memory" is subject to so many influences, the researchers commonly recommend that eye witness identifications
be regarded as a form of trace evidence: a fragment collected at the scene of
a crime, like a fingerprint or blood smear, whose integrity and reliability need
to be monitored and assessed from the point of its recovery to its ultimate
presentation at trial.[60]

Those working in the social sciences are not the only ones to question
the accuracy and value of testimony. The church has also shied away
from such practices within the past four decades. Professor Keith Drury,
the only person to have written on the subject of testimony from the
perspective of worship, speaks of the decline of the practice in smaller,
free denominations. The Wesleyan-Methodist Church, in particular, saw
a radical decline in the practice of testimony as the clergy became more
professionalized.[61] While many holiness churches used to conduct services for songs and testimonies, these slowly dwindled as the clergy
became more educated and desired to take back the pulpit from the laity,
who had a habit of hijacking services with unreliable or unedifying testimonies. While nothing has been published on the decline of testimonies, particularly within the Wesleyan Church, there are those who
will speak of the slow decline of the testimony as it was pushed from the
Sunday-morning worship service to the midweek service, to the holiness
campgrounds, to the testimony's final resting spot around the campfire
at the last night of camp. Even these campfire testimonies are too risky
for some. A youth pastor from the Midwest explained to me how he was
hesitant to continue with these fireside testimonies because, he said,
"kids will say anything in the dark," implying that as the lights dim so
does the veracity of the testimony.[62]

How do we discern true testimony from false? How can we trust that
what is testified to is akin to what actually happened? There is some baggage
that comes with a term like *false witness*. It conjures up images of intentional

---

[60]"Report of the Special Master," September 2008, www.judiciary.state.nj.us/pressrel/HENDERSON
%20FINAL%20BRIEF%20.PDF%20%2800621142%29.PDF.

[61]Keith Drury, interview by Amanda Drury, written record, Starbucks, Marion, Indiana, September 9, 2010.

[62]Chopper Brown, interview by Amanda Drury, written record, Riverside Bible Camp, Amherst,
Wisconsin, July 1, 2009.

deception and manipulation. And while there are those testifiers who are intentionally deceptive and seek to mislead, Coady reminds us it is quite possible for a testimony to be sincere and well intended yet entirely false.[63] Others may find themselves intentionally or unintentionally exaggerating particular details. Some may speak truthfully of an experience yet speak falsely when they attempt to discern or explain the experience.

Then there are those who give a verifiable testimony with verifiable commentary, but what they share is either completely inappropriate or not germane to the subject at hand. Pastor Charlie Alcock described an evening of testimonies in which a high school boy stood up and testified to the freedom he experienced from cutting (self-mutilation)—certainly a positive story of hope to uphold. Everything he shared was verifiable—the counseling he sought, the accountability from loved ones and so on. However, he included in his testimony such a graphic explanation of *how* one could physically go about self-mutilating that his words became inappropriate. Instead of focusing on the freedom from self-mutilation, teenagers were getting a detailed tutorial on how they too could cut.[64] Just because what is said is true, does not mean it is a testimony. And even if the true story spoken is a testimony, it does not mean it should be shared publicly (as we shall see in chapter five). And then there are those teenagers who are eager to "testify" in front of their peers, but instead of speaking of God they end up sharing a highlight from yesterday's football game. According to Coady, this kind of talk is not a true testimony: "It is not testimony unless it is relevant to the case being tried."[65] It is not testifying to announce to jurors what you are wearing if your wardrobe is not pertinent to the case being tried.

> **Just because what is said is true, does not mean it is a testimony. And even if the true story spoken is a testimony, it does not mean it should be shared publicly.**

So how can we best discern whether or not a testimony is pertinent? There are at least two factors that assist testing the authenticity of the testimony: community and time.

Community. Perhaps most important, the community offers account-

---

[63]Coady, *Testimony*, p. 57.
[64]Alcock interview.
[65]Coady, *Testimony*, p. 30.

ability to the testifier. It is often the community that helps differentiate between an authentic and false testimony. As mentioned earlier, no one is a solitary character in his or her own story. We are surrounded by others who take part in our story. Since our story is intertwined with others' stories, there is an element of authentication that emerges. This means I am not only accountable to those with whom my story inter-locks; they are also accountable to me.[66] MacIntyre writes:

> To be the subject of a narrative that runs from one's birth to one's death is, I remarked earlier, to be accountable for the actions and experiences which compose a narratable life. It is, that is, to be open to being asked to give a certain kind of account of what one did or what happened to one or what one witnessed at any earlier point in one's life than the time at which the question is posed . . . to say of someone under some one description ("The prisoner of the Chateau d'If") that he is the same person as someone characterized quite differently ("The Count of Monte Cristo") is precisely to say that it makes sense to ask him to give an intelligible narrative account enabling us to understand how he could at different times and different places be one and the same person and yet be so differently characterized. *Thus personal identity is just that identity presupposed by the unity of the character, which the unity of a narrative requires. Without such unity there would not be subjects of whom stories could be told.*[67]

All members of a community belong to one another's stories. As a result, one of the jobs of the community is to hold what is said accountable to the community's understanding of truth.

All members of a community belong to one another's stories. As a result, one of the jobs of the community is to hold what is said accountable to the community's understanding of truth. And so when Dr. Thorpe announced that God told him to leave his wife, the com-munity pushed back, challenging Dr. Thorpe on his testimony.[68]

Not only does the community hold the testifiers accountable to the *content* of their testimony, the community also holds them accountable to

---

[66]MacIntyre, *After Virtue*, p. 218.
[67]Ibid., pp. 217-18. Emphasis mine.
[68]Sadly, Dr. Thorpe ignored the advice of the community and followed through with his plan. His story took many unfortunate turns, including drugs, losing his medical license, bankruptcy and two failed marriages. There is no doubt in his former community that Dr. Thorpe's testimony was in fact a false witness.

the way they live *after* their testimony is given. A testimony can be well intended and true in content, but if testifiers do not live into the truth they have spoken, there is a hypocritical element to their testimony. The role of the community in this situation is to admonish them to live according to what they shared. So the man who publicly testifies he is 150 days sober will answer to his community when he is seen with a glass of wine in his hand.

A testimony can be well intended and true in content, but if testifiers do not live into the truth they have spoken, there is a hypocritical element to their testimony.

Time. There are also testimonies given that sound so radical to the community that they are unable or unwilling to substantiate the claims made. Coady describes correspondence between a friend of his and Captain Brett Hilder, a sea trader among the islands of the West Pacific for more than thirty years. Hilder spent twenty years of his life studying and documenting a strange phenomenon he witnessed beneath the surface of the water. His documentation described "a phosphorescent phenomenon he had occasionally seen from the bridge of his ship which took the form of long radial lines like the spokes of a wheel, radiating from a point anticlockwise. The phosphorescence was not on the surface but appeared to be 10 to 20 feet down, and seemed to pass directly under the ship with no diffraction or other effects."[69] Hilder carefully documented these observations, giving dates, latitude and longitude, and so on. He even stopped his ship on occasion to experiment with whether or not his ship was somehow responsible for the strange activity he witnessed. All of this was written up in a manuscript and submitted to various academic journals for publication where it was summarily rejected. The reason for the refusals to publish? Hilder's findings sounded fictitious.[70] Hilder was referring to something the rest of the scientific world was not yet ready to acknowledge. It was not until further evidence emerged with time that Hilder's findings were confirmed.[71] Despite the accuracy of Hilder's manuscript, the passage of time was needed in order to find further corroboration.

---

[69]Coady, *Testimony*, p. 190.
[70]Ibid.
[71]*The German Oceanographic Journal* later declared this phenomenon to be due to underwater seismic activity. Ibid., p. 191.

Gamaliel, a Pharisee from the first century, argued the need for time upon hearing the testimony of the apostle Peter. In a successful attempt to calm the angry Pharisees calling for Peter's death, Gamaliel addressed the Sanhedrin saying,

> Men of Israel, consider carefully what you intend to do to these men. Some time ago Theudas appeared, claiming to be somebody, and about four hundred men rallied to him. He was killed, all his followers were dispersed, and it all came to nothing. After him, Judas the Galilean appeared in the days of the census and led a band of people in revolt. He too was killed, and all his followers were scattered. Therefore, in the present case I advise you: Leave these men alone! Let them go! For if their purpose or activity is of human origin, it will fail. But if it is from God, you will not be able to stop these men; you will only find yourselves fighting against God. (Acts 5:35-39)

> **We are best able to thrive spiritually when we can articulate our narratives in a meaningful way. This is done in conjunction with our community, who helps construct, maintain and strengthen our personal spiritual identity.**

It is difficult to refute a testimony when the speaker claims her words are "from God." In some circumstances it may be prudent for the community to simply suspend judgment and allow for a greater passage of time to ensue.

To summarize, without a story an identity suffers. Whether or not they realize it, those who are unable to articulate their story face disruption to their identity. The same can be said for their spiritual identity. We are best able to thrive spiritually when we can articulate our narratives in a meaningful way. This is done in conjunction with our community, who helps construct, maintain and strengthen our personal spiritual identity.

All of my arguments thus far for an articulacy theory of testifying revolve around pragmatic, instrumental reasons: testifying helps form our spiritual identity, therefore we should testify. In the next chapter, I'll focus on my primary argument—that regardless of these pragmatic reasons, there are normative reasons for testifying. In other words, Christians should and must testify.

4

A Theology of Testimony

Christians are called to testify. Jesus did not leave any written documents as evidence to his identity. He left no sworn statements or winsome apology delineating the Christian life. Instead, Jesus sent witnesses. "You will be my witnesses in Jerusalem, and in all Judea and Samaria, and to the ends of the earth," he instructs his disciples (Acts 1:8). And instead of leaving them proper documentation, Jesus instead promises a living, breathing Spirit to empower and inform their testimonies.[1] It is clear that from the beginning Jesus intends for the good news to pass on through the testimony of witnesses empowered by the Holy Spirit, whether these testimonies are written down as Scripture or passed on by word of mouth. When the Holy Spirit came at Pentecost, it also ensured that this story would translate to various languages and cultures. From the start, Jesus intended for his followers to *testify* to the good news.

We testify not only because it is a spiritually formative practice but also simply because God calls us to do so. Jesus ascended into heaven in sight of eleven witnesses. These eleven men, combined with the women and men who witnessed the life, ministry, death and resurrection of Jesus, testified to God incarnate in such a way that the world saw Christianity spread from one hundred twenty believers in the months following the crucifixion to just under

> **Jesus did not leave any written documents as evidence to his identity. He left no sworn statements or winsome apology delineating the Christian life. Instead, Jesus sent witnesses.**

---

[1]Darrell L. Guder, *The Continuing Conversion of the Church* (Grand Rapids: Eerdmans, 2000), pp. 65-66.

thirty-four million in the year A.D. 350.[2] What prompted this explosion? Holy Spirit–inspired testimony.

We are indebted to the testimonies of early Christians. This commission of our Lord, however, was not limited to his eleven disciples, nor to the broader audience of eyewitnesses. We, too, are called to testify. The body of Christ is commissioned to witness. We are both permitted and obliged to testify. Testimony as witness is the lifeblood of the church today. We testify as evidence that God did not limit his in-breaking to the biblical world. We testify today because God did not withdraw his presence following the early church. God is just as present in our world as he was in the apostle Paul's world. And this same God commissions witnesses to testify to his ongoing, continued presence.

> This commission of our Lord, however, was not limited to his eleven disciples, nor to the broader audience of eyewitnesses. We, too, are called to testify.

This chapter has a single aim: to convince the reader that Christians are called to testify. This is a big claim and one that deserves careful attention. I intend to argue this claim through a theology of testimony that revolves around the work of Karl Barth and Phoebe Palmer. These two are unlikely bedfellows, as will be seen, but for a myriad of reasons, theirs are the two voices necessary for constructing a theology of testimony. Bringing these two theologians into conversation, I will build my central thesis that Christians are called to testify. I will also provide four subpoints to support this claim: First, Christians are to testify out of *gratitude* to God for the glory of his name. Second, not only are Christians called to testify, we are *empowered* to testify. Third, testifying is the primary *means* by which the church has evangelized and continues to evangelize today. Finally, testifying serves as a *seal* of retention for that which God has graced us.

> God is just as present in our world as he was in the apostle Paul's world. And this same God commissions witnesses to testify to his ongoing, continued presence.

Up until this point my arguments have focused on pragmatic reasons

---

[2]Rodney Stark, *The Rise of Christianity: A Sociologist Reconsiders History* (Princeton, NJ: Princeton University Press, 1996), pp. 5, 7.

for testimony: testimony shapes our identity, testimony can serve as a kind of legitimating apparatus, testimony helps construct "soft reality." What emerges after a careful study of Scripture as well as examining the Christian traditions is a much more normative claim: *Christians are called to testify.*

CONSTRUCTING A THEOLOGY OF TESTIMONY

When contemplating the relationship between theology and testimony, an appeal to narrative theology might seem logical.[3] However, even a small glimpse into the world of narrative theology produces murky results for a multitude of reasons. The concept of narrative theology today contains a great deal of baggage. The narrative theology that skyrocketed in the 1960s and '70s, both in its Yale and Chicago forms, has lost some of its momentum as a theology unto itself. This demise is perhaps due to its intangible nature. L. Gregory Jones explains, "There is not so much a distinct position known as 'narrative theology' as there is a variety of ways in which theologians have argued for the significance of narrative for theological reflection."[4]

---

[3]Or "postliberal theology," as it is called by some.

[4]L. Gregory Jones, "Narrative Theology," in *The Blackwell Encyclopedia of Modern Christian Thought*, ed. Alister E. McGrath (Oxford: Blackwell, 1999), p. 395. There are a number of ways to understand narrative theology, which is one of the reasons why it is difficult to jump into this kind of theology. The unclear contours of this theology are what prompted those theologians originally interested in narrative theology to see the concept as passé or incoherent. Most theologians still dealing with the concept of narrative theology have simply absorbed it into other theological understandings rather than dealing with it as a standalone theology. H. Richard Niebuhr's *The Meaning of Revelation*, often seen as a key text within the narrative theology corpus, is largely interpreted in various ways. Niebuhr's work is especially helpful for the ways in which he links confession and history: "As we begin with revelation only because we are forced to do so by our limited standpoint in history and faith so we can proceed only by stating in simple, confessional form what has happened to us in our community, how we came to believe, how we reason about things and what we see from our point of view" (H. Richard Niebuhr, *The Meaning of Revelation* [Louisville, KY: Westminster John Knox Press, 2006], p. 21). Other theologians vocal on the subject of narrative theology include Brevard Childs, Stanley Hauerwas, Stephen Crites, Alasdair MacIntyre, Johann Baptist Metz and L. Gregory Jones. We readily see the influence of Hans Frei as well as he mediates Barth to his students. Some speak of the emerging church as having absorbed much of the narrative theology talk. At the risk of being reductionistic, narrative theology tends to speak to the necessity of Christian theology, drawing from the Bible in order to focus on a narrative portrayal of faith as opposed to a set of propositions drawn from Scripture. Currently, some understand narrative theology to determine how we interpret Scripture or preach from the pulpit. Others see narrative theology as an invitation to join our own life stories into a greater story found within Scripture. This latter understanding has been particularly prevalent among some in the emerging church movement. Mars Hill Church of Grandville, Michigan (not to

What *is* consistent within narrative theology, however, is the primacy of story, particularly as it relates to collateral commitments. For the theologian, this means primacy of story over systematics. For the philosopher, primacy of story over law. For the Christian educator, primacy of story over theory.

The instincts that prompted this interest in narrative theology are certainly worth exploring, particularly when we focus these instincts on the concept of testimony. Those who have written on the subject often trace their lineage from Hans Frei back to H. Richard Niebuhr, and finally to Karl Barth (though it should be noted that neither Niebuhr nor Barth actually used the term *narrative theology*). Jones speaks of Barth and Niebuhr in particular as being discontent with the emphasis the Enlightenment placed on "isolated, objective facts, which seemed to privilege science and marginalize theology. They turned to the significance of narrative as a way of explicating theological convictions."[5] Instead of relying on dogmatic assertions, theologians like Barth appeal to the narrative presentation of faith as it appears in Scripture and throughout history. Jones explains, "Barth was primarily concerned to understand Scripture in its witness to God. He did not propose a method for reading Scripture as a narrative. Rather, he displayed such a reading in his theological treatment of various doctrines, arguing that central Christian teachings are best understood in narrative terms."[6] In other words, rather than explicating a theory or method of narrative theology, Barth allowed what he understood as the narrative nature of the gospel to set the parameters and serve as inspiration for his work.

Rather than delving further into the internal arguments of narrative theology, I will instead focus on two narrative theologians: Phoebe Palmer and Karl Barth (though it is important to note that neither one referred to themselves as such). By calling them narrative theologians, I

---

be confused with the Mars Hill of Seattle), claims an understanding of narrative theology at the core of its identity: "We believe that, as a community and individuals, God is calling us to participate in God's unfolding story of love, rescue, resurrection, and restoration. Our Narrative Theology Statement embeds our beliefs in context, perpetually inspiring our community to participate in what God is doing in our world" (http://marshill.org/believe/about/narrative-theology).

[5]Jones, "Narrative Theology," p. 395.

[6]Ibid.

appeal to Palmer's history as a Methodist revivalist deeply committed to helping Christians access and articulate their own spiritual narratives as a continuation of the narratives found within Scripture. I also draw from Karl Barth as a Christocentric, confessional theologian of witness.

I will continue by engaging the topics of narrative theology with a look at the narrative motivations and underpinnings of Barth's theology, combined with the testimonial writings of Phoebe Palmer, which will be helpful in constructing my own theology of testimony. So while my theology of narrative identity is informed by modern theologians who have dealt with narrative theology, my interaction will primarily be with the fount of this discussion: Barth, as well as the nineteenth-century evangelist Palmer.

A Theology of Testimony: Karl Barth and Phoebe Palmer

Bringing confessional, Reformed Barth and revivalist, Methodist Palmer together in conversation may initially appear to be a theological concoction of oil and water. Both, however, dedicate much of their work to the subject of testimony or witness. And while I can appeal to my own narrative as a Wesleyan holiness student who studied at Princeton Theological Seminary as rationale for intermingling Barth and Palmer, the truth of the matter remains that in order to offer a serious look at the theology surrounding testimony, neither Barth nor Palmer can be neglected. Though they view testimony from different angles, the insights they provide concerning the role and function of testimony cannot be denied or ignored in my argument for a theology of testimony. One of the benefits of approaching the practice of testimony from the perspective of practical theology is that we are able to step back and look at not just the inner logic of these two theologians but also the normative guidance these figures have provided to a concrete practice as it exists in a particular, North American context. In the sections ahead I will highlight how the pair relate to one another and the practice of testimony.

Why Phoebe Palmer? Within a few decades of her death, Palmer was all but forgotten save for holiness preachers. Some suggest her gender had something to do with the lack of honor. Others shied away from her mysticism. Still others saw her as a simple derivative of John Wesley.

Palmer is often caricatured in Wesleyan holiness circles as a laywoman whose theology is fraught with wishful or magical thinking. Those who desire holiness need only "name it and claim it" as a kind of positive confession.

Recent scholarship by Elaine Heath of Southern Methodist University, however, places Palmer at the cornerstone of the American holiness movement.[7] Heath identifies Palmer as a modern-day mystic for the Methodist tradition.[8] Palmer is important in my development of a theology of testimony because of her lifelong commitment to the practice of testimony. Testimony is at the cornerstone of Palmer's understanding of sanctification, making her one of a handful of theologians who has taken the concept of testifying seriously and written to that effect.

Palmer is best known for her promulgation of entire sanctification. Claiming to be prompted by John Wesley's writings and supported by Scripture, Palmer set forth her "altar theology" or "the shorter way" to achieve the gift of sanctification.[9] At the risk of oversimplifying her work, Palmer encourages Christians to partake in three steps to move toward sanctification: entire consecration, faith and testimony. Palmer's understanding of sanctification comes from Romans 12:1-2:

> I beseech you therefore, brethren, by the mercies of God, that ye present your bodies a living sacrifice, holy, acceptable unto God, which is your reasonable service. And be not conformed to this world: but be ye transformed by the renewing of your mind, that ye may prove what is that good, and acceptable, and perfect, will of God. (KJV)

Palmer latches onto this understanding of a "living sacrifice" and believes holiness to be a daily decision to lay one's life on the altar in an ongoing and dynamic manner. While my desire is not to endorse Palmer's theology carte blanche by any means, this mother of the North American holiness movement deserves serious examination when it

---

[7] Elaine A. Heath, *Naked Faith: The Mystical Theology of Phoebe Palmer* (Eugene, OR: Pickwick, 2009), p. 1.

[8] Ibid., p. 2.

[9] "Palmer's use of the term 'shorter way' does not the imply absence of process or journey. Nor does the phrase necessarily imply instantaneousness over process. Rather, the word 'shorter' underscores the potential for entering the way of holiness sooner rather than later, and gives a method for entering the way of holiness" (ibid., p. 93).

comes to the subject of testimony, as she understands the practice to be entirely necessary for Christians.

Why Karl Barth? About a decade after Palmer's death, the Swiss theologian Karl Barth was born, and his later work would profoundly shape the way we understand theology. It may seem counterproductive to bring Barth into a conversation arguing for the role of personal testimony in the life of the Christian. Theologian John Drury explains how Barth unrelentingly criticized the practice of personal testimony. His entire project is directed against the move to make one's own personal spiritual narrative the proper object of theological reflection. He is the apotheosis of the Reformed instinct to turn away from one's self and toward God and God's glory. He carries this instinct to its logical conclusion by critiquing his own tradition for making too much of self-abnegation, which functions as a twisted sort of negative natural theology. So Barth's critical potential with regard to personal testimony is indisputable.[10]

With that said, however, Barth's entire project revolves around the concept of *Zeugnis*, which we translate as "testimony" or "witness." This leads Drury to the conclusion:

> Theology itself participates in the Christian community's service of witness by testing its contemporary proclamation against its own norms. Even in this critical function, theology is itself testimony in a different discourse. So, although he is a great critic of the personal testimony, Karl Barth is *the* theologian of Christian witness.[11]

With Barth's theology, we can say that the role of the Christian is to witness—or testify—on behalf of Jesus Christ to the world.

The preceding paragraphs introduce a new term in this discussion: *witness*. In some contexts, *testimony* and *witness* function interchangeably. In legal circles the two words are used differently, so we hear about a witness who takes the stand to testify, implying that the witness is a person and the testimony is what that person says. The witness testifies. Witness

---

[10]John L. Drury, "Barth and Testimony," in *Karl Barth and the Future of Evangelical Theology*, ed. Christian T. Collins Winn and John L. Drury (Eugene, OR: Pickwick, 2014), pp. 102-14. In the interest of full disclosure, John Drury is my husband.

[11]Ibid.

is who we are; testify is what we do. This distinction does not necessarily work in the church—particularly in evangelical circles where one might speak of sharing his testimony or "witnessing" to a friend. Many mainline churches appear to be more comfortable speaking of "witness" than "testimony." Clearly, the relationship between the two words is ambiguous.

Is Jesus calling us to testify or to witness? Which is it? Does it matter? What is the relationship between the two words? Etymologically speaking, both words come from the *mart*-word family, which appears in words like *martys, martyria, martyrion, martyrein* and *diamartyresthai.*[12] This *mart*-word family is not easily translated into English.[13] Missiologist and theologian Darrell Guder explains: "We find ourselves unable to maintain the common unity of the *mart* root in English and we must render the original with both 'witness' and 'testify/testimony' and their various meanings."[14] Does it matter? Perhaps not, although Guder sees this ambiguity as beneficial, as it reminds us "that witness in the biblical sense is multidimensional, a comprehensive definition of Christian existence."[15]

At first glance, *witness* and *testify* are terminological equivalents; however, witness seems to take on a broader function in Christian circles, including inarticulate acts, while testimony has a narrower meaning attached to verbal narration. I will address this issue further in the final chapter.

Are Palmer and Barth compatible? At first glance, Palmer and Barth are not obvious conversation partners. In fact, in some areas they are

---

[12]Guder writes: "It is missiologically provocative that this word family includes terms for the person who is the witness (*martys*, mainly in Acts), the testimony rendered by the witness (*martyria, martyrion*), and the process of giving or bearing witness (*martyrein, diamartyresthai*). This cluster of meanings indicates that Christian witness defines the identity of the Christian (thus, Karl Barth speaks of 'the Christian as witness'), the impact of such persons within human experience (their testimony), and the dynamic process of living out witness" (Guder, *Continuing Conversion of the Church*, p. 55). Guder is referring to Karl Barth, *Church Dogmatics* IV/3.2 (Edinburgh: T & T Clark, 1962), pp. 554-614, especially pp. 608-10; hereafter cited as *CD* IV/3.2.

[13]"Testimony" derives from the Latin *testis* (a witness who testifies or swears on his virility—as proof of his honesty). The significance of *testis* is disputed among scholars. Some claim a man swearing an oath would literally place his hand on his testicles to swear on his livelihood. Florence explains this word "was later absorbed into the Greek *marturia* (the witness as 'martyr' who swears his or her life). ... In the most literal and corporeal sense, testimony is passionate truth-telling" (Anna Carter Florence, *Preaching as Testimony* [Louisville, KY: Westminster John Knox Press, 2007], p. xxi).

[14]Guder, *Continuing Conversion of the Church*, p. 70.

[15]Ibid.

diametrically opposed. I imagine both would balk at the thought of being paired with the other. Palmer was suspicious of any kind of systematized theology: "It has been my aim to avoid most carefully every thing like a display of theological technicalities," she writes, favoring instead "to follow the simple Bible mode of teaching."[16] I have little doubt Palmer would have been turned off by the magnum opus that is *Church Dogmatics*. Palmer's critique of "theological technicalities" contains even more bite when she claims that such "theological hair-splittings and technicalities" actually *hindered* her spiritual progress until she "resolved to let all these things alone."[17] All Palmer claimed to need was "the simple, naked word of God" as her guide.[18] She referred to herself as a "Bible Christian" and refused to accept the title theologian.

Barth, on the other hand, would have been horrified by the amount of subjectivity in Palmer's work. The emphasis on individuals sharing their personal encounter with God with others would no doubt be problematic in Barth's eyes considering his warning that a Christian's personal liberation is fragmentary, exemplary, indirect and subordinate.[19] Furthermore, I can only imagine Barth's dismay at the thought of his theology being used to argue for sharing a personal narrative (as will continue to be discussed throughout this chapter).

Despite these major differences, both figures speak of Jesus Christ as having a personal, transformative effect on individual lives and the following necessity to witness or testify to this effect. Palmer's understanding of God breaking into individuals' lives is somewhat assumed and intuitive in her writing. Her reluctance to engage in systematized theology keeps her from clearly spelling out such an assertion, but her work is fraught with examples and illustrations of how and where God intersects the personal lives of individuals.

Barth speaks of "the personal liberation of the Christian" as "an indispensable presupposition, a *conditio sine qua non*, of his existence as a

---

[16]Richard Wheatley, *The Life and Letters of Mrs. Phoebe Palmer* (New York: Garland, 1984), p. 509.
[17]Charles Edward White, *The Beauty of Holiness: Phoebe Palmer as Theologian, Revivalist, Feminist, and Humanitarian* (Grand Rapids: F. Asbury Press, 1986), p. 105.
[18]Ibid.
[19]*CD* IV/3.2, pp. 651, 655, 656, 674.

witness of Jesus Christ and therefore of his Christian status."[20] The Christian who has experienced this "personal liberation" must "attest to the world that the light of the act and revelation of God in Jesus Christ is not a dream, nor an illusion, nor a subject of mere theory, but a fact, and indeed a fact which is relevant and significant for each and every man."[21]

Both Barth and Palmer agree on the transformative effect Jesus Christ has on the individual, personal life. Where they disagree is in *how* that individual is to relate to the world. It is at this point of digression where Barth and Palmer might inform and correct the other's argument.

Why Palmer needs Barth. While Palmer speaks freely of her central commitment to Jesus, the ways in which she conceives of testimony often focus on the speaker to a fault. According to Palmer, following justification we encounter sanctification, which can be achieved through three steps (this is commonly known as Palmer's altar theology or "the shorter way"): (1) complete consecration to God, (2) faith that this consecration has taken place and, finally, (3) testifying to the sanctification that has come as a result of consecration and faith. Much of Palmer's Christology is assumed or intuitive, and her altar theology is easily interpreted as being too dependent on the individual. Sanctification is the "golden ring" on the carousel that simply requires one to lift an arm and grab.

---

[20]Drury continues to shed insight on Barth's relationship with testimony by highlighting various passages within *CD* IV/3.2 from his essay on "Barth and Testimony" referred to earlier in this chapter: "The incidental-yet-indispensable pairing and its equivalents recur throughout." See the following statements from *CD* IV/3.2, §71.6 regarding the personal dimension or experience of liberation: "The personal significance of vocation for the Christian is a phenomenon which only accompanies the ministry [*Dienst*] of witness [*Zuegnis*] which properly makes him a Christian. . . . Nevertheless, this personal aspect must not be ignored nor dismissed too summarily. The Christian does have his own existence in relation to what he has to attest as such" (p. 648); "incidentally perhaps, but unavoidably, all these things are also to their own judgment and salvation" (p. 650); "as he can be concerned only with the ministry [*Dienst*] required of him, he will incidentally, without any desire, longing or effort, yet quite infallibly, have a care for his own best interests" (p. 653); "all this, even the very best of it, is only incidental. . . . But . . . it is inevitable" (p. 654); "we have defined and understood this as something incidental and additional, as a by-product of the real thing which makes him a Christian, of his appointment as a witness. But this cannot mean that it is an unimportant and even dispensable determination of Christian existence" (p. 655); "the incidental but necessary question of the existential determination of the Christian by the content of his witness" (p. 655); "its relative necessity" (p. 656); "his little personal liberation, his own faith, knowledge and experience, are an indispensable prerequisite, a *conditio sine qua non*" (p. 657); "I myself as a Christian . . . am an indispensable instrument to myself as a theologian, as a preacher and pastor, as the witness which I am to be like others. But I am not a theme or object" (p. 677).
[21]Barth, *CD* IV/3.2, p. 658.

Furthermore, Palmer's aversion to "theological technicalities" prevents her from developing systematic criteria for a *responsible* practice of testimony. Palmer's focus on accepting one's testimony in faith leaves little room for a testimony to be challenged, as one's doubt can be considered a sign of weakness. One can only wonder if her lack of criteria contributes to the demise of testifying as a practice in the twentieth century due to abuse and misuse.

Barth is clear that one's witness always points to that which is outside of and prior to oneself. Speaking of Barth's explanation of the Christian witness, John Drury explains: "The Christian's witness is at its heart not about her and her experience of salvation, but about God and God's reconciliation of the world to himself in Jesus Christ. Therefore, one's own personal liberation is incidental to the task of testifying to this reality."[22]

Again, Barth speaks of the Christian's personal liberation as fragmentary, exemplary, indirect and subordinate.[23] These kinds of qualifications add an element of humility to people's testimony as they recognize they have but a loosely held fragment of belief. Additionally, these kinds of qualifications may in fact open them up to receive input from others and prompt them (and their community) back to the Scriptures in order to provide further clarification and direction.

Barth also gives Palmer a kind of holy awe that is missing from her work. Palmer's call to testify is so strong and insistent that sometimes her readers are left with the impression that the *act* of testifying is more important than the *content* of the testimony or the *subject* of the testimony. She instructs those who are unsure of what they might say at a testimony service to simply stand up and open their mouths and speak anyway.[24] She bases this, albeit out of context, on Psalm 81:10, "Open wide your mouth and I will fill it." Sorely missing from Palmer's work, which Barth certainly provides, is the paradox of being commanded to speak of God combined with the knowledge of one's own unworthiness and inability to speak of God.[25] Adhering to Palmer's practice of testimony without a

---

[22]Drury, "Barth and Testimony," p. 110.
[23]Barth, *CD* IV/3.2, pp. 651, 655, 656, 674.
[24]White, *The Beauty of Holiness*, p. 110.
[25]I discuss this later in this chapter.

Barthian corrective leaves us with an inwardly turned practice that leaves little room for accountability and a wide margin for abuse.

Why Barth needs Palmer. Barth explicitly condemns the sharing of a personal testimony. "The personal liberation of the Christian can and should fit him for this ministry of witness," he writes, "but it cannot and should not become the content of his witness. The servant has to proclaim his Lord and His work and Word, not himself nor the process by which he has become His servant."[26] Barth's fear is that he could only "obscure the light of the real theme of my witness if I tried to put myself forward as a transparency, no matter how fine or profound my experiences." Barth continues: "He must spare his fellows any direct information concerning himself and the way in which the Word of God has become significant and effective in his own life in some such application."[27] We witness, but we do not share our personal experiences. Our personal liberation is what makes us *fit* for the role as witness, but this personal liberation is not the *content* of our witness.

Barth appears to have a particular person or group in mind when he offers these warnings against personal sharing: "It need hardly be indicated against what kind of proclamation this delimitation is directed," he writes.[28] It could be he is reacting against the grave abuses he had witnessed and overreacts, erring on the side of cutting out one's personal experiences entirely. Most likely, Barth is speaking against Pietism, particularly in its German and Swiss expressions.[29] According to Darrell Guder, the point of the section under question

> is not the validity of the experience but dwelling on it in one's testimony as though the point of the gospel was that one should have that experience. Since Barth has clearly underlined in [previous sections] that the Christian vocation is witness, and that witness points to God's grace in Christ, it is not appropriate to turn the direction around and point to oneself, as Pietism did (and does).[30]

---

[26]Barth, *CD* IV/3.2, p. 676. Barth does speak of a witness with a "personal edge," but what this looks like is vague.

[27]Barth, *CD* IV/3.2, p. 677.

[28]Ibid.

[29]Eberhard Busch, *Karl Barth and the Pietists: The Young Karl Barth's Critique of Pietism and Its Response*, trans. Daniel W. Bloesch (Downers Grove, IL: InterVarsity Press, 2004).

[30]Darrell Guder, email message to the author, November 8, 2011.

We see a small overlap with Palmer's work at this point. For all of the critiques one might raise against Palmer and her sometimes sloppy use of experience, she was extremely critical of anyone holding up an experience as a norm to be experienced by all. Palmer did not experience a kind of radical conversion. She claims to not be able to pinpoint a moment of conversion and could not garner the emotions she saw others exuding concerning their faith. Speaking of herself in the third person, she says that she "felt like weeping because she could not weep, imagining if she could plunge herself into those overwhelming sorrows, and despairing views of relationship to God, spoken by some, she could then come and throw herself upon his mercy with greater probability of success."[31] After continually comparing her own conversion story to the more dramatic conversion stories of others, Palmer claimed experiences could be dangerous because an individual could fall into the trap of trying to obtain the same experience as another Christian. This desire to keep from norming one's experience prompted Palmer's strong language used earlier concerning being a "Bible Christian." Palmer resolved to not trust in others' experiences but only "naked faith in the naked word of God."[32] Of course, Palmer leaves much more room for the sharing of personal experiences than Barth, who seems to restrain the practice.

Drury offers a compelling response to Barth's barring of personal experience:

> Although I would concur with Barth that one's personal liberation is only fragmentary in form, exemplary in function, and subservient to the task of witness, I do not find Barth's absolute rejection of personal testimony compelling. Instead, I would take the remainder of his delimitations as criteria for evaluating the adequacy of a given testimony. A personal testimony that would satisfy these delimitations might be rare, but it is not absolutely inconceivable, and so Barth's absolute gag rule is unjustifiable. Better to root out abuse than to bar

---

[31]Phoebe Palmer, *The Way of Holiness with Notes by the Way: Being a Narrative of Religious Experience Resulting from a Determination to Be a Bible Christian* (New York: Palmer & Hughes, 1981), pp. 73-74.

[32]This was a phrase Palmer frequently used in her writings, hence the title of Heath's aforementioned book, *Naked Faith: The Mystical Theology of Phoebe Palmer*. For more evidence, see Palmer, *Way of Holiness*, p. 87, and Phoebe Palmer, *The Promise of the Father* (New York: Garland, 1985), p. 7.

use. It seems to me one's indispensable personal liberation, however incidental it may be, would at least occasionally make its way into public proclamation.[33]

While I appreciate Barth's fear of obscuring "the light of the real theme of" a person's witness if he were to share his personal experience with God, there is much of what Barth is calling the witness to do that is still unclear to me. So while the witness is to avoid "direct information concerning himself," Barth also obliges the witness to testify with a "personal edge," a charge that is somewhat ambiguous.[34] According to Guder, Barth's strong but ambiguous statements concerning personal experience appear to shift as he grows older, making these claims somewhat milder. This topic, Guder admits, deserves further scholarship.[35]

> **If I withhold what I understand to be an encounter with God, I am not allowing the body of Christ to speak into my experience. If my experience with God remains private, the church can neither confirm my experience nor question my experience, meaning that it is quite possible for me to go through life either (a) unsure of whether or not what I encountered was of God or (b) with a faulty understanding of how God interacts with the world.**

Part of Barth's hesitation concerning speaking publicly of one's experience seems to be the *difficulty* of doing so: "It is obviously technically impossible to speak of [personal liberation] with any precision or in a way which will be illuminating and useful to others."[36] I agree that this kind of speech is difficult; to say it is impossible, however, may be too strong of a statement. Is not Paul's sharing of his Damascus road experience a testimony to his personal liberation, which Barth references in this section of the *Dogmatics*? Certainly God is the subject, but Paul's experience is in no way lost in the narration.

---

[33]Drury, "Barth and Testimony," pp. 111-12.

[34]Barth, *CD* IV/3.2, p. 676.

[35]In an email to the author on November 8, 2011, Guder offers further explanation: "One further insight arising from my current doctoral seminar, working on the theological legacy of John Mackay: Mackay was a strong advocate of Barth's theology but had concerns about Barth's critique of Christian experience. But he does note that Barth's later work seemed to be making a shift in this regard. It's actually a theme that would merit more research. There is also some valuable insight on this in Barth's conversations (the *Gespräche* volumes in the Gesamtausgabe), where similar questions are directed to Barth in an informal setting. He is milder in his remarks there."

[36]Barth, *CD* IV/3.2, p. 676.

Yes, there are dangers involved in speaking publicly of one's experiences with God. However, we might also say there are dangers involved in *not* speaking publicly of one's experiences with God. If I withhold what I understand to be an encounter with God, I am not allowing the body of Christ to speak into my experience. If my experience with God remains private, the church can neither confirm my experience nor question my experience, meaning that it is quite possible for me to go through life either (a) unsure of whether or not what I encountered was of God or (b) with a faulty understanding of how God interacts with the world. Should not our experiences with God be subjected to the authenticating scrutiny of the church?[37] First John 4:1 instructs us to "not believe every spirit, but test the spirits to see whether they are from God, because many false prophets have gone out into the world." There exists a kind of responsibility to discern communally that which one claims is from God.

I imagine if Palmer could address Barth on this issue she would direct him to the countless personal testimonies found within Scripture (many of which he refers to in the section on witness/testimony). Indeed, Palmer sees her call for testimony as nothing new, but merely a continuation of a biblical precedent.[38] As we shall see later in this chapter, Palmer also makes a convincing case for the necessity of testifying for the edification of others. This charge seems to be echoed in Barth's writings, making his warnings to restrain from personal testimony even more ambiguous.

A Theology of Testimony

Bringing the writings of Palmer and Barth into conversation with one another, I want to continue the construction of a theology of testimony by focusing on four important points related to Christians' call to testify: (1) Christians testify out of *gratitude* to the glory of God; (2) Christians

---

[37]Think again of the story of Jake in the previous chapter who initially wanted to challenge the congregation to give 80 percent of their lives to the Lord.

[38]In *Pioneer Experiences*, a book of testimonies edited by Palmer, Rev. Bishop Janes provides an introduction where he explains that the content of the book is not new or novel experiences. "On the contrary," he writes, "they profess to be illustrative and confirmatory of what predecessors in all ages of the Church have enjoyed and declared" (Rev. Bishop Janes, introduction to *Pioneer Experiences*, by Phoebe Palmer [New York: Garland, 1984], p. 5).

are *empowered* to testify; (3) testimony is and always has been the Christian's primary *means* of witness; and (4) testifying serves as a *seal* of one's experience and understanding of God. There is a temporal element to these subpoints that can be seen briefly in table 4.1 and that will be explained at length in the remainder of this chapter.

Table 4.1. Temporal Overview of a Theology of Testimony

	Past	Present	Future
God	**Gratitude**—we offer gratitude for that which God has done in the past	**Means of grace**—the practice of testimony serves as a means of grace in our present situation	**Glory**—we testify in order to give God the glory due his name
Humanity	**Tradition**—the Christian tradition is one of testimony and witness	**Seal**—what we articulate can serve as a kind of "seal" of our experience	**Witness**—we testify for the sake of those who have yet to respond to the gospel

Earlier chapters have argued for testimony from a sociological and psychological standpoint. We should testify because testifying can serve as a legitimizing apparatus as well as a way in which we can construct our identity. My argument for testimony, however, runs deeper than the social sciences. The thesis of this chapter is simple: *Christians are called to testify*. We are permitted and even obligated to speak of God. Testifying is good for the church and is *required* of the church. Testimony is not the "cherry on top," but the substance of our sustenance as people of faith.

In the Gospel of Luke a crowd begins to praise Jesus upon his entrance to Jerusalem on Palm Sunday. "Blessed is the king who comes in the name of the Lord! Peace in heaven and glory in the highest!" (Lk 19:38). Some Pharisees instruct Jesus to rebuke those speaking. Instead, Jesus tells the Pharisees, "I tell you, if they keep quiet, the stones will cry out" (Lk 19:40). The implication is that not only does Jesus deserve our praise, Jesus *must* be praised and *will* be praised in one way or another.

This kind of witness is not limited to adults and inanimate objects. After he tells of Jesus' clearing of the temple, Matthew tells of children shouting praises to Jesus in the temple courts. "Do you hear what these children are saying?" the chief priests and teachers of the law asked. "Yes," replied Jesus, quoting Psalm 8:2, "From the lips of children and infants you, Lord, have called forth your praise" (Mt 21:16). From infants to adults we are all called to testify. Some might argue, "This is praising, not testifying." There is overlap, and I will discuss the distinction between praising and testifying in the following chapter. But for now, suffice it to say that these are people who have a personal encounter with Jesus in their everyday lives and are called and commissioned to publicly articulate their responses.

Others might argue, "Forget for a moment whether or not we are *obliged* to testify; we must first ask whether it is *possible* to testify. How can we testify of a transcendent God?" While we may have been made in the image of God, there is nevertheless a Creator-creature distinction. What is more, we speak from a fallen state about that which is perfectly holy. How can we possibly find the words worthy of such a task? In agreement with this question, Barth declares: "We ought to speak of God." This normative statement is followed up with the recognition, "We are human, however, and so cannot speak of God. We ought therefore to recognize both our obligation and inability and by that very recognition give God the glory."[39]

When speaking of the divine attributes, Barth addresses God's self-disclosure and self-concealment: "He is at one and the same time knowable and unknowable to us. . . . At every point, therefore, we have to be silent, but we have also to speak."[40] There is a tendency for Christians to emphasize either God's transcendence or God's immanence at the expense of the other. Those who focus on God's transcendence may prematurely give up on any pursuit of knowing this God. But the knowledge of God, Barth writes, "must not be swallowed up by the ignorance," nor must our pride allow for the knowledge of God we do have to overpower that which we do not know of God.[41] God's revelation makes two demands of us: "the obedience of knowledge and the humility of ignorance."[42] We must simultaneously speak and be silent.

We see this dilemma take form in the calling of the prophet Isaiah. Seeing the Lord exalted upon the throne surrounded by heavenly beings declaring God to be holy, Isaiah cries out that he is a man of unclean

---

[39]Karl Barth, *The Word of God and the Word of Man*, trans. Douglas Horton (New York: Harper, 1957), p. 186.

[40]Karl Barth, *Church Dogmatics* II/1 (Edinburgh: T & T Clark, 1957), p. 342; hereafter cited as *CD* II/1.

[41]Ibid.

[42]Ibid., p. 342.

lips. Barth notes Isaiah declares that his *lips* are unclean, not his heart.[43] Barth explains:

> It is thus clear to him from the very first that what he has seen and heard demands to be expressed and proclaimed. It must go out as a human word on human lips, to be sounded forth and heard in its immeasurable positive and negative significance among all men throughout the earth. But he knows of no human mouth which is able and worthy to form and express that which corresponds to the matter. He must confess that he is a member of the community and people in which there are only unclean lips which contradict rather than correspond to the matter. He thus knows that what he has seen and heard must be expressed and yet cannot be expressed by a human mouth. It is in view of this dilemma that he cries: "Woe is me! For I am undone."[44]

We are simultaneously obliged to speak of God and unable to speak of God. Our lips must form the words that our mouths are unworthy of speaking.

We cannot fully know God. God is hidden. God is other. But, writes Barth, we must state with the same amount of vigor that "He becomes completely recognizable by us, not because of our capacity, thinking and speaking, but because of the grace of His revelation which we cannot refuse to receive."[45] God is present and allows us to witness his presence. How is it Isaiah can speak? How is it that we might speak? Grace. The presence of God and our ability to recognize the presence of God comes solely through grace. "It is by the grace of God and only by the grace of God that it comes about that God is knowable to us,"[46] writes Barth. "He gives Himself to us to be known, which establishes our knowledge of Him. God's revelation is not at our power and command, but happens as a movement 'from God.'"[47] Not only is God available to be known, Barth speaks of God's *readiness* to be known.[48] God may be other, but God desires to be known. God is eager to be known. God promises to be known—and God fulfills his promises.

---

[43]Barth, *CD* IV/3.2, p. 580.
[44]Ibid.
[45]Barth, *CD* II/1, p. 342.
[46]Ibid., p. 28.
[47]Ibid. "'God is knowable' means God can be known—He can be known of and by Himself; in His essence, as it is turned to us in His activity, He is so constituted that He can be known by us" (ibid., p. 65).
[48]"There is readiness of God to be known as He actually is known in the fulfillment in which the knowledge of God is a fact" (ibid.).

While we certainly cannot grasp the fullness of God, that which we do witness *is truly God*. Barth explains that God encounters humanity in such a way that "in this encounter He still remains God, but also raises man up to be a real, genuine knower of Himself."[49] This is what we were created for: to know and love God. God allows us to know him:

> God makes Himself known and offers Himself to us, so that we can in fact love Him as the One who exists for us in such a way that it is obvious that He Himself will be loved by us because He offers us reason and cause to love Him. And it consists finally in the fact that God creates in us the possibility—the willingness and readiness—to know Him; so that, seen from our side also, there is no reason why this should not actually happen.[50]

We can know God—we can truly know the true God. And as a result, we are both authorized and compelled to witness of this God.

While some might grant the claim that Christians are to speak of God, they might question whether the Christian needs to be a part of that story. Why not just speak of God without a personal narrative attached? Would not it be better for us to leave ourselves out of the story and focus entirely on God? To locate our talk of God within the realm of our own personal experience seems to reek of anthropocentrism.

We must affirm that God chooses to be known with and among us. In the Old Testament, God often reveals himself within our own personal histories. And when God introduces himself to individuals God often does so by indicating God's relation to the person being addressed. "I am the God of your father," God says to Moses at the burning bush, "the God of Abraham, the God of Isaac and the God of Jacob" (Ex 3:6). And with these words God identifies himself as a God that is involved in Moses's personal history. Only secondarily, when Moses pushes him for a clearer name, does God respond, "I AM WHO I AM" (Ex 3:14). To know God is to know God in relation to us. God has chosen to be known among us. Transitioning to the New Testament we see God's self-revelation first and foremost through God's Son, Jesus Christ. Even the name Jesus is given, "Emmanuel," meaning "God with us" highlights God's apparent desire to

---

[49]Ibid., p. 32.
[50]Ibid., p. 33.

be known among humanity within our own histories. To speak of differentiating between God's story and our stories is to see a kind of false competition between the two narratives. God exists without humanity but has chosen to dwell among humanity. The God we worship has chosen to be known with us, and we may and must testify to God according to his revelation in our personal histories.

That we can truly encounter God is a gift of grace. We cannot manipulate ourselves into encountering the true God. We receive God's presence as a gift. And what is the proper response to a good gift? Gratitude.

WE TESTIFY OUT OF GRATITUDE TO THE GLORY OF GOD

Gifts are neither earned nor repaid; they are freely given. And the proper response to the gift of God's presence is gratefulness. Palmer proposes that to deny God our gratefulness is to rob God of the glory due his name. She directs us to the healing of the ten lepers in Luke 17. To not gratefully acknowledge the work of God is to cast one's lot with the nine former lepers who do not return to thank Jesus. "Were not all ten cleansed? Where are the other nine?" Jesus asks (Lk 17:17). The question Jesus poses implies an assumption that surely those healed would return in gratitude. Because gratefulness, of course, is the fitting response to a good gift.

Palmer explains that those who have been "cleansed through the blood of the lamb" and are "unwilling to glorify Christ openly" are guilty of "base ingratitude towards their Divine Cleanser."[51] Here Palmer pauses to critique those churches that do not approve of testifying. Whereupon the congregants are kept from testifying, claims Palmer, the "Lord is *robbed of the glory* due to His name."[52] Providing further credence to the necessity of testifying, Palmer appeals to the Scripture she claims is "divinely enjoined, '*Give* unto God the glory due unto His name'" (Ps 29:2 KJV).[53]

This charge to give God the glory he deserves does not necessarily paint an attractive picture of God. On the contrary, true as Palmer's claims may be, God sounds somewhat like a disgruntled grandmother demanding a thank-you note following the giving of a birthday gift. It

---

[51]Palmer, *Pioneer Experiences*, p. xi.
[52]Ibid.
[53]Ibid.

should be noted, however, that God does not *need* our gratitude. Nothing that we give God provides him with something he is lacking. God is complete within himself. However, while God is complete in himself, he has chosen to dwell among us. God does not need our gratitude—it may be a fitting response, but God is not dependent on it; rather, God desires it *for our sakes.* As a Creator who has chosen to be for us, a response of gratitude has a positive, formative effect on our spiritual identity. We offer gratitude to God, God resides in our praises, and we are blessed in return. This kind of acknowledgment is not grounded in obligation but is organically found within a grammar of gratitude that is deeply embedded within loving relationships. A thank you is a fitting and natural response to a gift of love. We express gratitude not to satisfy God's ego but to live into our proper identity as creatures called and blessed by God.

The self-giving nature of God is such that even in our gratitude we are blessed.

When we "give God the glory due his name," we foster a spirit of humility. We recognize that God is working and that the fount of every good and perfect gift comes from above. Grateful acknowledgment keeps us from wrongly assuming we are responsible for good gifts. This kind of humility shapes our understanding of our own human identities in relation to the divine. We see the goodness of God. We are formed by gratitude. We come to know who we are on a deeper level because of gratitude. This humbling gratitude further elucidates self-knowledge as well as knowledge of the divine. Testifying gives God the glory due his name. Testifying increases our own self-knowledge and shapes our identity.

But the act of testifying does something more than just cultivate the virtue of humility. The self-giving nature of God is such that even in our gratitude we are blessed. While there is certainly a gift of humility that comes with this kind of thankful acknowledgment, the blessings continue. Consider again the story of the ten lepers Palmer refers to. We might say that the one man who returned to thank Jesus grew in the virtue of humility and properly acknowledged his own weakness and dependence on God. But there was another gift embedded in his act of thanks. This man was the only one who got to experience the actual, physical presence of Jesus Christ. The ten lepers that called out to Jesus for pity did so at a distance. The man that returned to thank him, we read, "threw himself at Jesus' feet and thanked him" (Lk 17:16). All ten were healed, but only one of these men actually got to spend time in Jesus' presence. When we thank God, we are moved from experiencing his gifts on the periphery, and we are able to experience his gifts at his very feet. Intimacy with God is not found in God's gifts; it's found in God's presence.

Intimacy with God is not found in God's gifts; it's found in God's presence.

Of course, we can experience the presence of God without having to articulate that presence. God's presence is mediated to us through various gifts—consider the Eucharist, where God's presence is mediated through the bread and wine. God's presence is mediated to us in various ways at various times, and even if we do not speak of this presence we may still experience a kind of implicit faith. When we do articulate this presence, however, we bear witness to the identity of this gift giver. We need narrative in order to render an identity. Perhaps God is present in his gifts, but his identity can and must be testified to. Christ is present in his gifts, yet his identity is not known if his story isn't told.

Jesus doesn't wait for the lepers to be thankful before he offers healing; his gifts are not conditional. He heals both the grateful and the ungrateful. God gives good gifts not because we say thank you. God gives good gifts because God is good. Thanks be to God.

But what if we do not *feel* grateful? What then? Those in the Wesleyan tradition are often fond of quoting the advice Peter Bohler gave John Wesley to "preach faith until you have it, then because you have it you will preach faith."[54] Wesley is *invited* to preach this faith despite what he sees as his own spiritual shortcomings. We testify to the glory of God with the hope and understanding that any sense of obligation or rote gratitude will eventually attune our spirits into being grateful people as we "taste and see that the Lord is good" (Ps 34:8). There are many ways in which this testimony might take place. We are not required to testify through rose-colored glasses, downplaying suffering and forcing praise

---

[54]John Wesley, *The Journal of John Wesley*, ed. Hugh Price Hughes and Percy Livingstone Parker (Grand Rapids: Christian Classics Ethereal Library, 2000), p. 49, www.ccel.org/ccel/wesley/journal .pdf.

in some kind of display of religious grit. Certainly there are times in our lives where the proper testimony is one of lament. What is important is to say *something*—to take spiritual stock of one's life and speak accordingly. Our testimonies give credit where credit is due. Our testimonies cultivate within us the virtue of humility. And ultimately, our testimonies usher us into the presence of the Lord. God's grace not only makes it possible for us to testify by bringing us into God's presence and eliciting our gratitude; God is present in the testimonies themselves by empowering them through the Holy Spirit.

Consider the apostle Paul's conversion experience on the Damascus road. The gift of his conversion (frightening as it may have been) comes along with a call—to proclaim Jesus Christ. It is with this example in mind that Barth argues that conversion itself is neither a private experience nor a private gift.[55] Barth explains that while Paul's personal salvation was "no doubt very dear to him," it was only secondary to his larger call, with his main concern being "his function as a witness."[56] Paul's conversion cannot be separated from his "calling, commissioning and sending."[57] Paul's conversion was enmeshed with his call to witness. His call to witness was not a gift subsequent to his conversion; his conversion and call were one in the same. Paul was both invited and commanded to witness.

Of course, I am using perhaps the greatest Christian witness in history to make a normative point. What does Paul's call to witness have to do with us? Just because Paul testifies does not mean we should testify. *I am no Paul*, some might say, *I don't aspire to be an apostle, not even one "abnormally born"* (1 Cor 15:8). Though Paul was certainly anointed in his witness we have no reason to think his witness is the exception. Paul is not the exception; his is a normative calling. "I urge you to imitate me," he writes in 1 Corinthians 4:16. Barth explains:

> But if Scripture is normative and is to be followed in this matter, where else are we to seek that which makes a Christian of the man called to be a Christian except along the lines of the mode of existence of the biblical prophets and

---

[55]Here again we see ambiguity concerning Barth's charge to keep from sharing the content of one's personal liberation.

[56]Barth, *CD* IV/3.2, pp. 591, 593.

[57]Ibid., p. 592.

apostles? And in what can it be found or consist but that in his own order and place, and therefore without aspiring or being able to be a Moses or Isaiah, a Peter or a Paul, he will be very clearly and definitely set in the ranks with these, being made a witness in analogy, however distant to them?[58]

The invitation and the charge to testify are not limited to Paul, nor are they tasks limited to clergy. We are all invited to participate in this practice that both glorifies God and serves as witness to our communities. Writing along similar lines, Palmer directs her reader to commentator Dr. Scott who writes:

> Every servant of God is a witness for him; and they all can give such an account of what he has wrought in them, shown to them, and done for them, as to lead others to know, believe, and understand His power, truth and love; and the help which He sends in answer to their prayers, enables them to testify that He never faileth those who trust in Him.[59]

We are to carry on the practice of speaking publicly of God. Palmer understood the practice of testifying as carrying out a biblical precedent. In *Pioneer Experiences*, Rev. Bishop Janes explains in his introduction that the contents of the book are not new or novel experiences. "On the contrary," he writes, "they profess to be illustrative and confirmatory of what predecessors in all ages of the Church have enjoyed and declared."[60]

The presence of God is a gift. When we testify to this gift, we do so not only to thank and glorify God, nor solely to "seal" in our experience, but also for the sake of others. God gives gifts and these gifts are seldom private. The gift may be for the believer, but it is not *only* for the believer. God's gifts, Palmer writes, "must be diffused or lost.... A light put under a bushel goes out, and then it neither enlightens ourselves nor others."[61] Palmer scholar Elaine Heath speaks of generative gifts of God. These gifts are to be given away: "No experience of God is meant simply as a private gift. Everything in the believer's life is to have a larger impact on the world."[62] There is a clear missional aspect to this kind of gratitude.

---

[58]Ibid., p. 593.
[59]Palmer, *Pioneer Experiences*, p. xi.
[60]Ibid., p. 5.
[61]Phoebe Palmer, *Full Salvation: Its Doctrine and Duties* (Salem, OH: Schmul, 1979), p. 71.
[62]Heath, *Naked Faith*, p. 107.

Palmer refers her readers to the commentator Matthew Henry, who writes:

> What God has wrought in our souls, as well as for them, we must declare to others. . . . God's people should communicate their experiences to teach others; we should take all occasions to tell one another the great and kind things God hath done for us, especially to our souls, the spiritual blessings.[63]

That which has affected us, he continues, we should use to try to affect others.[64] Referring to an "ascent" into spiritual maturity, Palmer claims that Christians are ordained to testify to their journey. Recognizing that there are those who falter along their way, Palmer directs her reader to "show others who would ascend, the foot-marks by which you ascended."[65] For although there are those whose feet have been taken "out of the horrible pit and out of the miry clay . . . they have scarcely begun to make the ascent." And Jesus, our "forerunner," has ordained us to illuminate the path that we have trod. We testify to the "experimentally tested . . . solidity of those foot-marks, by which [we] have thus far ascended."[66] We are grateful for the footmarks left by others throughout the centuries and are invited to participate by articulating the paths by which we ascend.

CHRISTIANS ARE EMPOWERED TO TESTIFY

We are not called to testify and left on our own to figure it out for ourselves; we have been given an advocate. This is certainly a gift, as the task of testifying is daunting. We are commissioned to testify. We *may* speak of God and we *must* speak of God, but we must also acknowledge that we cannot speak accurately of God. This tension has the potential to fill us with anxiety. If Isaiah, the great prophet, trembled at the thought of testifying, what of those of us who do not consider ourselves to be prophets? How can I know that which I speak is truly of God?

God calls us to be his witnesses to the ends of the earth. This is not an empty call, however. What God *calls* us to do, God also *equips* us to do. How do we know what to testify? How do we receive the confidence that

---

[63]Palmer, *Pioneer Experiences*, p. viii.
[64]Ibid.
[65]Ibid., p. vii.
[66]Ibid.

our testimony is true and begs articulation? We see within Scripture a twofold empowerment that comes from the Holy Spirit. First, the Holy Spirit testifies to our spirit that we are children of God, thereby empowering our testimony through personal conviction. Second, Jesus promises that the Holy Spirit will provide us with the necessary words for our testimonies. Again, this comes alongside the 1 John 4:1 charge to "test the spirits," which once more highlights the ways in which God often uses the community of believers to help us discern that to which we testify.

We see the Holy Spirit present in testifying in at least two distinct ways. First, the Holy Spirit testifies to our spirits as to our spiritual identities, and second, this same Spirit empowers the testimonies we share.

The Holy Spirit testifies to our spirits. When Jeff awoke from his accident he had his community nearby to teach him his role and identity in society. He was re-introduced to family, friends, his occupation and, ultimately, his relationship with God. Jeff readily acknowledges his indebtedness to his community. Jeff's community, however, was not the only voice speaking into his identity. Before friends and family even uttered a word to Jeff, the Holy Spirit was testifying to Jeff's spirit that he was a child of God. Before Jeff even had the ability to grasp the concept of a child, the Holy Spirit was at work articulating and forming Jeff's identity.

Jeff's testimony on this subject is lengthy but well worth reading:

> At the time of my memory loss I definitely felt like a blank slate. As I reread and re-explored what spirituality was, let alone Christian faith, I felt [at the time] as though I was logically making the decisions and taking the steps towards growth. . . . Faith was an absolutely foreign and unthinkable concept . . . so as I read and researched I went with what made sense. Out of all I read (the *Qur'an*, etc.) the Bible made sense. As I grew and my little memory-less world became bigger, more faith-full, and God-experiencing, I never looked back.
>
> In retrospect, although I couldn't feel, see, hear, taste or touch the Holy Spirit, I am now thoroughly convinced the Holy Spirit was ministering to me the entire time. As I came to understand my call to ministry (and as it was described to me by others), I became convinced that even in this tragic loss of memory I *couldn't* have chosen anything else.
>
> Regardless of experiential feelings or occurrences, in retrospect, the Holy Spirit was testifying to, teaching me about, and reminding me of the God who

had saved, loved, adopted, bought and paid for my soul. Without the Holy Spirit I'm not sure that I ever would have come back to Him, even though at the time, I thought I was the one deciding upon these things.

In that way the Holy Spirit absolutely used every resource at his disposal to help me reconnect to my identity in Christ. From the simple urging of my heart to the "homework" my pastor gave me to the stories of my relatives to the conversations with old friends and church members to things that are so commonplace in our world that I don't even remember at this point. All that says nothing of my wife. Heather's love and dedication had to have been God-breathed. Nobody without His indwelling and listening to His spirit could have put up with all she did to help me recover.[67]

The apostle Paul writes, "The Spirit himself testifies with our spirit that we are God's children" (Rom 8:16). Because the Spirit testifies to our condition as children of God we can have the confidence to speak boldly of the Father who is slow to anger and rich in love (Ps 145:8). What is more, as we see evidenced in Jeff's testimony, the Spirit testifies to our spirit in and through the testimony of the community.

We can explore how testifying has a spiritually formative effect on our identity. We can examine how talking about faith makes us more faithful. But the truth of the matter is, before a word of testimony is on our lips, the Holy Spirit has been testifying to our own spirit, speaking into and forming our identity—preparing us in such a way that we might have the spiritual eyes to catch a glimpse of where and how God might be at work in our lives, and empowering us to testify to that effect. Anything true and good concerning God that comes from my lips has its origin in the Holy Spirit testifying to my spirit.

Anything true and good concerning God that comes from my lips has its origin in the Holy Spirit testifying to my spirit.

This is what John Wesley calls the "witness of the Spirit." Contemplating the words of Romans 8:16, Wesley wonders aloud *how* the Holy Spirit testifies to our identity. "It is hard to find words in the language of men to explain 'the deep things of God.' Indeed, there are none that will adequately express what the children of God experience," he writes. "But

---

[67]Email from Jeff Brady to the author, June 22, 2014.

perhaps one might say . . . the testimony of the Spirit is an inward impression of the soul, whereby the Spirit of God directly witnesses to my spirit, that I am a child of God; that Jesus Christ hath loved me, and given himself for me; and that all my sins are blotted out, and I, even I, am reconciled to God."[68] Our spirits testify as a response to the Spirit's testimony. We find the courage to speak of a transcendent God because of the Spirit's testimony to our relationship with this God. It is worth noting that this is one of the places where Palmer widely differs from Wesley. While Wesley speaks of the Spirit being the first to testify, Palmer speaks of the Spirit *responding* to our testimonies. "In proportion as I testify of the cleansing blood to others, so does the Spirit testify in my own experience."[69] While Palmer claims to be furthering Wesley's work, it is at this point where she sorely needs a corrective from her predecessor.

This same Spirit that testifies to our spirits also testifies to the Son's relationship to the Father. John alludes to the testimonial relationship of the Holy Spirit in John 15 when Jesus informs the disciples of the coming Advocate whom he will send from the Father. This "Spirit of truth who goes out from the Father," Jesus says, "will testify about me" (Jn 15:26).

Perhaps the most illuminating scriptural passage concerning the testimony of God is found in 1 John 5. John begins with an appeal to three witnesses: "This is the one who came by water and blood—Jesus Christ. He did not come by water only, but by water and blood. And it is the Spirit who testifies, because the Spirit is the truth. For there are three that testify: the Spirit, the water and the blood; and the three are in agreement" (1 Jn 5:6-8). There is much debate among Bible scholars as to the meaning of water and blood. Some suggest the water represents Jesus' baptism and

---

[68]John Wesley, "The Witness of the Spirit," in *The Works of John Wesley, Volume V* (Grand Rapids: Baker, 1978), p. 115. Wesley writes: "That this testimony of the Spirit of God must needs, in the very nature of things, be antecedent to the testimony of our own spirit, may appear from this single consideration: We must be holy of heart, and holy in life before we can be conscious that we are so; before we can have the testimony of our spirit, that we are inwardly and outwardly holy. But we must love God, before we can be holy at all; this being the root of all holiness. Now we cannot love God, till we know he loves us. 'We love him, because he first loved us.' And we cannot know his pardoning love to us, till his Spirit witnesses it to our spirit. Since, therefore, this testimony of his Spirit must precede the love of God and all holiness, of consequence it must precede our inward consciousness thereof, or the testimony of our spirit concerning them" (ibid., pp. 115-16).
[69]White, *The Beauty of Holiness*, p. 114.

the blood his death. Others see the two as an allusion to Jesus' death where in John 19:34-35 both water and blood came from Jesus' pierced side. While there is not a consensus among scholars as to the meaning of the water and blood, John is eager to provide his readers with three witnesses to testify to Jesus. John goes on to explain:

> We accept human testimony, but God's testimony is greater because it is the testimony of God, which he has given about his Son. Whoever believes in the Son of God accepts this testimony. Whoever does not believe God has made him out to be a liar, because they have not believed the testimony God has given about his Son. And this is the testimony: God has given us eternal life, and this life is in his Son. Whoever has the Son has life; whoever does not have the Son of God does not have life. (1 Jn 5:9-12)

The testimony here is the experience of redemption—of new life in Christ. Peter appeals to the testimony of the Spirit in the Jerusalem Conference of Acts 15. Peter addresses the apostles and the elders, acknowledging that the Gentiles appear to be filled with the Spirit. The Gentiles, Peter claims, are participating in eternal life, which is the true testimony from God.

John's speaking of the three that testify offers an important point to ponder—especially for those who are skeptical of whether a human testimony is truly of God. John has carefully pointed out the three witnesses that confirm the testimony. If God is concerned with providing additional witnesses to confirm God's work, Christians have every reason to hope that others will confirm that which they believe is from God as well. God appears to be more than willing to provide multiple witnesses to testify to his work.

Raymond Brown makes an important observation concerning the Greek used to describe the testimony the Father gives concerning his Son: to testify "on behalf of" (*peri*) occurs in verses 9 and 10 as well as sixteen other times in the Gospel of John. Other than that it is rarely found in the New Testament.[70] He goes on to explain the tense of the verb as

> perfect (and there will be three more perfect tenses in v. 10), so that God's testimony was clearly given at some time in the past, either in the ministry of Jesus (5:6) or in the conversion of the readers when they were begotten as

---

[70]See Acts 22:18; 23:11. Raymond Edward Brown, *The Epistles of John* (Garden City, NY: Doubleday, 1982), p. 587.

God's children. The range of the perfect tense, however, leaves open the possibility that the testimony continues to have effect in the present.[71]

The Trinity testifies to the works and deity of the Father, Son and Holy
Spirit. More specifically, the Holy Spirit *today* testifies to our spirits that
we are children of God. Not only do we have this prevenient testimony,
we also have the witness of Scripture which Jesus claims offers testimony
to himself (Jn 5:39). This practice of testifying is not limited to the Trinity
or the Holy Scriptures. Those who understand themselves to be disciples
of Christ are also called to testify. And we have every reason to hope that
God will confirm true testimonies through the words and actions of
others. The Holy Spirit testifying to our relationship with God as God's
children holds vast implications so far as our personal identity is concerned. Our truest self is that to which the Holy Spirit testifies. The Holy
Spirit testifies to the fullness of who we were created to be—children of
God and heirs with Christ. We have the greatest sense of personal identity
when we are attuned to the testimony of the Holy Spirit.

But how do we go about *hearing* the testimony of the Spirit? It is here
where words fail us. Wesley is circumspect when it comes to describing
what this testimony looks like:

> The manner how the divine testimony is manifested to the heart, I do not take
> upon me to explain. Such knowledge is too wonderful and excellent for me:
> I cannot attain unto it. The wind bloweth, and I hear the sound thereof; but I
> cannot tell how it cometh, or whither it goeth. As no one knoweth the things
> of a man, save the spirit of a man that is in him; so the manner of the things
> of God knoweth no one, save the Spirit of God.[72]

There does not seem to be any formulaic answer concerning how to
hear from the Holy Spirit, though we see evidence in Scripture of God's
pleasure in providing multiple witnesses to confirm his testimony, as we
shall shortly see.

---

[71]Ibid.
[72]Wesley, "The Witness of the Spirit," p. 117. Wesley continues: "How can we keep from deceiving
  ourselves that it's not just our natural mind telling us we are children of God? It is certain, one who
  was never convinced of sin, is always ready to flatter himself, and to think of himself, especially in
  spiritual things, more highly than he ought to think. . . . How then may the real testimony of the
  Spirit with our spirit, be distinguished from this damning presumption?" (ibid.).

True testimony is empowered by the Holy Spirit. The second form of Holy Spirit empowerment has more of an external than an internal role. The Synoptic Gospels speak of the Holy Spirit as providing the words of our testimony. Jesus instructs his disciples not to worry about what they will say when they are arrested and brought to trial: "Just say whatever is given you at the time, for it is not you speaking, but the Holy Spirit" (Mk 13:11). This Holy Spirit, who fell at Pentecost, blessing all cultures and all languages, is the empowering force behind the testimonies that have shaped the church throughout the centuries. And all through the Scriptures, the testimonies we read from the saints of the past appear to be Holy Spirit empowered. Whether it is Stephen's testimony prior to his martyrdom, Paul's on Mars Hill or Philip's four daughters, we see evidence throughout Scripture of the empowerment of the Holy Spirit in the testimonies of ordinary people.

Paul writes the Corinthians: "For in him you have been enriched in every way—with all kinds of speech and with all knowledge—God thus confirming our testimony about Christ among you" (1 Cor 1:5-6). Not only are we given the words and knowledge for the content of our testimony, God himself confirms the words the Spirit gives. This kind of confirmation may come through affirmation found in Scripture, through our community, or through a still, small voice. Regardless of how it comes, the testimony that is from God is always consistent with the character of God as lived out by Jesus Christ.

Testimony is and always has been the Christian's primary form of witness. Testimony is a normative Christian practice. "When the Advocate comes," Jesus says to his disciples, "whom I will send to you from the Father—the Spirit of truth who goes out from the Father—he will testify about me" (Jn 15:26). But the Holy Spirit is not the only one who testifies. Jesus gives further instructions to his disciples: "And you also must testify, for you have been with me from the beginning" (Jn 15:27). While

> **Our very word *testimony* is tightly related to our understanding of martyrdom.**

faith is a gift of God, the content of that faith has been passed on to us from the cloud of witnesses. And so though we might not have witnessed Jesus raising Lazarus from the dead, Lazarus's sisters did. And because of their testimony we know that Jesus has power over death. We may not have seen Jesus calm the wind and the waves on the Sea of Galilee, but the disciples did, and thanks to their testimony we know that even the wind and the waves are subject to his word. What we know of the life, death and resurrection of Christ Jesus is what was witnessed to by the early church and confirmed and preserved by the Holy Spirit.

To be a Christian in the early church was to testify—even if it meant one's death. The *mart*-family words discussed at the beginning of this chapter are the backbone of our word for "martyr." Our very word *testimony* is tightly related to our understanding of martyrdom. The concept of testifying, however, came *before* the concept of dying for one's faith. Barth favorably quotes H. Strathmann: "Stephen is not called a martyr because he dies, he dies because he is a witness of Christ."[73] Those martyrs who held more tightly to their testimony than their life have profoundly shaped the church. Or, as Tertullian says, "The blood of the martyrs is the seed of the church."[74] We are indebted to the testimonies of the early Christians, and we dishonor their sacrifice when we resist testifying.

As mentioned earlier, Jesus did not leave written documentation for his followers; he left us the testimonies of eyewitnesses empowered by the Holy Spirit. Christians today are dependent on the testimony of the Spirit given through the martyrs and great cloud of witnesses. Richard Bauckham highlights Christianity's reliance on the category of testimony for the content and *telos* of our faith.[75] Furthermore, it is the category of testimony, Bauckham claims, "that enables us to read the Gospels in a properly historical way and a properly theological way. It is where history and theology meet."[76]

Bauckham goes on to speak of the "neglected fact that all history, like all knowledge, relies on testimony."[77] He is leery of historical criticism that sterilizes Christian theology to accept only that which has been unequivocally proven.[78] Too often, he writes, historical criticism and

---

[73]Barth, *CD* IV/3.2, p. 611, as taken from Gerhard Kittel and Otto Bauernfeind, *Theologisches Wörterbuch Zum Neuen Testament* (Stuttgart: Kohlhammer, 1949), p. 498.

[74]Tertulian, *Apology*, trans. T. R. Glover (Cambridge, MA: Harvard University Press, 1984), chap. 50.13, p. 227. Literally, *semen est sanguis Christianorum*, or "The blood of Christians is seed."

[75]Bauckham is well connected with the narrative theology conversations. Richard Bauckham, *Jesus and the Eyewitnesses: The Gospels as Eyewitness Testimony* (Grand Rapids: Eerdmans, 2006).

[76]Ibid., pp. 5, 6.

[77]Ibid., p. 5.

[78]Here we see traces of narrative or postliberal theology in the desire to move away from histori-

Christian theology part ways: the former constructing "a historical Jesus based only on what they can verify themselves by critical historical methods," the latter relying solely on what is read in the Gospels for "our access to the Jesus in whom Christians believe."[79] Bauckham understands testimony to breach the rift between critical historicism and Christian theology. Testimony, he claims, is what allows these two to work alongside one another. He writes:

> I suggest that we need to recover the sense in which the Gospels are testimony. This does not mean that they are testimony rather than history. It means that the kind of historiography they are is testimony. An irreducible feature of testimony as a form of human utterance is that it asks to be trusted. This need not mean that it asks to be trusted uncritically, but it does mean that testimony should not be treated as credible only to the extent that it can be independently verified. . . . Trusting testimony is not an irrational act of faith that leaves critical rationality aside; it is, on the contrary, the rationally appropriate way of responding to authentic testimony. Gospels understood as testimony are the entirely appropriate means of access to the historical reality of Jesus.[80]

In other words, "the category of testimony enables us to read the Gospels as precisely the kind of text we need in order to recognize the disclosure of God in the history of Jesus."[81] And it is because of these very testimonies that we have access to the content of our faith.

We do not testify to anything radically new; rather, our words are a continuation of what has been testified to in the past. Our words keep moving the story forward through the guidance of the Holy Spirit. Guder speaks of the Holy Spirit continuing "the event character of God's actions into

> **We do not testify to anything radically new; rather, our words are a continuation of what has been testified to in the past. Our words keep moving the story forward through the guidance of the Holy Spirit.**

---

cal, dogmatic assertions and toward a narrative understanding of the gospel.

[79]Bauckham, *Jesus and the Eyewitnesses*, p. 5.

[80]Ibid.

[81]Ibid. "Testimony offers us, I wish to suggest, both a reputable historiographic category for reading the Gospels as history, and also a theological model for understanding the Gospels as the entirely appropriate means of access to the historical reality of Jesus" (ibid.).

every generation and age" through the witness of the gospel, which is "translated into [our] particular stories."[82]

This idea of translation is key in discussing what testifying looks like today. While we do not discover a new kind of truth in our words, our words will nevertheless sound different than those witnesses who have come before us. Robert Jenson explains that the gospel

> must change in order to remain gospel. In every generation and every culture the gospel is the story of Jesus told as the encompassing plot of that generation's story as it is living it. In every time the gospel must speak the language in which the men of that time interpret their lives to themselves. Nor does the gospel merely accommodate itself to history. It makes history. . . . In all its changes, the gospel remains itself. But it remains historically itself, as a person remains himself through the changes of his life—or rather, changes precisely in order to remain himself, and loses himself if he stops and clings to what he was. Indeed, the self-identity of the gospel is the self-identity of a person: different forms of words are the same gospel in that they are all about and in the name of the one, living and personally self-identical risen Jesus.[83]

Our testimonies today continue to make the presence and identity of God known within our particular contexts. The Spirit empowers our testimonies, allowing for crosscultural boundaries to be breached as we are enabled to speak to the hearts and minds of strangers (no doubt this is what we see happen at Pentecost as the same gospel was heard in different tongues for different people).

Testifying serves as a seal to one's experience. Palmer speaks of testifying as sealing in that which we have received from God. To not testify, she claims, is to risk losing that which we have received. She recounts the story of John Fletcher, who claims he lost the gift of sanctification four

---

[82]Guder, *Continuing Conversion*, pp. 65-66.

[83]Jenson explains further: "an intrinsic part of each occurrence of the gospel-communication is the birth of new language. . . . Precisely to be itself, the gospel is never told the same way twice. The formulas which yesterday opened Jesus' future will tomorrow bind to the past. 'We are justified by faith alone,' said Luther, and liberated four generations. When preachers say these words today, supposing themselves to be following Luther, they bind us to the terrible law of having to save ourselves by the quality of our sincerity, for that is what 'faith' has come to mean since the eighteenth century. And who knows what 'justified' might mean, without lengthy explanations" (Robert W. Jenson, *Story and Promise: A Brief Theology of the Gospel About Jesus* [Philadelphia: Fortress Press, 1973], pp. 11, 10).

or five times because he refused to testify to its manifestation.[84] When he decided to testify to this experience, both Fletcher and Palmer claimed a seal was placed on his life.

Palmer's understanding of sealing can be well understood through a comparison to the sealing of canned goods. Both seals keep contents from spilling forth. Seals not only prevent spillage, they also *preserve* the contents of the jar. When we testify, we are protecting and preserving that which God has given.

Palmer's discussion of sealing one's experience leaves me uneasy in how close it seems to come to a kind of works-righteousness. I'm not entirely comfortable with the carte blanche declaration that this is something we must do to seal a gift from God. While I am hesitant to hold up Palmer's story of Fletcher as normative in the retention of one's sanctification, I do think there is merit in exploring what a verbal seal might do. Does someone like Fletcher *have* to testify to keep the gift? No, I would argue, appealing again to the nine lepers who did not return to verbally express their gratitude. God gives good gifts not because we testify but simply because God is good.

> **Our testimonies today continue to make the presence and identity of God known within our particular contexts. The Spirit empowers our testimonies, allowing for crosscultural boundaries to be breached as we are enabled to speak to the hearts and minds of strangers.**

This does not mean, however, that words are not important. There are reasons for a man like Fletcher to articulate this gift as opposed to simply *acting* as if he has received it. What kind of reasons? Why can't Fletcher simply allow his "actions to speak louder than words," to use the old adage? Why are we called to testify? What about the Franciscan call to "preach the gospel at all times. If necessary, use words"?[85]

Throughout Scripture we see words being elevated. Creation comes about through a word. Before creation was spoken into being, however, there was "the Word," and this Word took on flesh and dwelled among us according to the apostle John (Jn 1:1). A Christian with actions and no words is akin to the husband who never tells his wife he loves her.

---

[84]Palmer, *Full Salvation*, p. 60.
[85]Though unproven, this is often attributed to Saint Francis.

He might bring her flowers on their anniversary and evenly share household responsibilities. He might show physical affection and offer appropriate tokens on special days. But despite these actions, something is missing when love is not verbally articulated. There is power in the spoken word; words *do* things. Again, J. L. Austin's speech-act theory reminds us of the power of words to cause and create change. Words spoken in a marriage ceremony actually create a married couple. The words spoken by a judge can actually acquit someone.[86] In short: words are necessary.

In the fifth chapter of Mark, Jesus is walking through a crowd when a woman subject to bleeding reaches out and touches his cloak, believing that if she can simply touch him she will be healed. Immediately, we read, her bleeding stops and she feels herself free from suffering. Not content with solely doing good, however, Jesus stops and asks for the person who touched him to be identified. Eventually the woman comes forward to explain the situation. Jesus simply responds, "Daughter, your faith has healed you. Go in peace and be freed from your suffering" (Mk 5:34). All that we see in Scripture attests to the understanding that Jesus' works and words go together. He does not simply heal; he articulates what has occurred. His words solidify himself as the fount of the healing and acknowledge the spiritual healing from sin that is not immediately evident to the naked eye. We see in the life of Jesus an undeniable link between words and actions. Words appear to be the capstone, or the seal, of the gift.

In the proceedings of the Western Union Holiness Convention, Phoebe Palmer continued her rationale for testifying, stating that not only was testifying essential

> to the promulgation of Christian holiness, but even more essential to the personal retention of that grace. One had to give public testimony in order to be "clear in his experience." Indeed if personal testimony lagged, it was one of the most certain signs of a lack of religious life which would finally culminate in complete apostasy.[87]

---

[86]Austin, *How to Do Things with Words.*

[87]Melvin E. Dieter, *The Holiness Revival of the Nineteenth Century* (Lanham, MD: Scarecrow Press, 1996), p. 36.

The public declaration of what God has done in one's life is, according to Palmer, an act that preserves and maintains precisely what it is God has done.

This understanding of sealing is not limited to some kind of intangible act of the Holy Spirit's; we can also understand this concept from a sociological standpoint. When we testify, those who receive our testimonies play a variety of roles. They seal our words by holding us accountable to that which we have shared. They seal our words by asking questions of clarification and potentially offering insights into our testimonies. The spiritual narrative threads of our lives do not occur to impersonal bodies, Niebuhr explains, "but to selves in community with other selves, and they must be so understood."[88] Within the community we see emerge a kind of stamp-of-approval as communities both "refresh and criticize each other's memories of what has happened."[89]

Worship professor and Wesleyan pastor Keith Drury recalls testimony services he attended as a child and the reoccurring seal-like language he encountered:

> It was often quoted in Scripture, "Believe in your heart, confess with your mouth." They put it that way. Okay, you believe, but it's the confession that settles the issue. It's the speaking it that makes it true. "Seal" and "stake." Growing up I heard people say "drive a stake" and I think the story my generation heard most often was the guy who kept having doubts about his conversion and the pastor got a stake and carved a date on the stake and he took it out behind the barn and the young man drove it in. And the pastor told him, "Every time the devil causes you to doubt, you bring him out here and point to that date and tell him he's wrong." Every time I heard "drive a stake" I heard that story. It was told by so many preachers and evangelists. You can come back to this moment and say I believe.[90]

From a psychological standpoint we seal our testimonies when we physically utter the words aloud. As discussed in chapter two, our articulated words become available to us in a new way. Our testimony is objec-

---

[88]H. Richard Niebuhr, "The Story of Our Life," in *Why Narrative?*, ed. Stanley Hauerwas and L. Gregory Jones (Grand Rapids: Eerdmans, 1989), p. 32.
[89]Ibid., pp. 35-36.
[90]Keith Drury interview.

tified in a new way that allows us to examine our words and hold them at arm's length for consideration. When we make our experiences concrete through the confines of articulated language, we are sealing our experiences. Externalizing something strengthens that which is internal.

This chapter revolves around the central thesis that Christians are called to testify. This strong statement begs the question, "What if Christians do *not* testify? Are they still Christians?" The Christian who does not testify is akin to a fish out of water, or perhaps, a fish in very shallow water. Living the full Christian life without witness is difficult indeed—our growth is stunted and we does not reach our potential. Can we be a Christian without testifying? Probably. Can we thrive in our relationship with God without testifying? I am suspicious of such a claim. Jesus Christ has purposed that his message be spread by word of mouth. We cannot speak of God, yet we must speak of God. The God we testify to is not one confined to a holy book, but bleeds out of our bound pages into our everyday lives, encountering his people and inhabiting their praises. The question regarding how this task is to be carried out is addressed in the next chapter.

> **When we make our experiences concrete through the confines of articulated language, we are sealing our experiences. Externalizing something strengthens that which is internal.**

5

Testimony in Practice

Toward a Practical Theology

One Sunday a couple years ago, my church gave space for testimonies during its morning worship service. While testimonies are regularly given in the youth group, it is unusual for this to occur in the main worship service. I felt my pulse quicken as the time for testifying unfolded.

It was New Year's Day, the first Sunday of 2012. One of the pastors on staff stood and invited those who were so inclined to stand and offer a two- or three-sentence testimony concerning where they had seen God at work in their life over the past year. I pulled out a notepad and prepared to take notes. I was nervous. Was anyone going to testify? If they did, were these testimonies going to be pertinent to the question asked? Would the testimonies turn into lengthy sermons? I wondered *who* was going to testify; honestly, I assumed those testifying would be in their sixties and seventies—congregants who may have regularly given witness during their early, formative years. What I saw brought me great joy.

Eight people testified, four women and four men. Their ages ranged from the early twenties to the late eighties. All eight testimonies were both appropriate and edifying. They all stayed within the length parameters given (two or three sentences), and all spoke explicitly of God's actions. One testimony neglected to contain a narrative kernel, prompting me to interpret her words as more of a confession of praise than a testimony in the strictest sense. But it was, nevertheless, edifying. One man praised the Lord for a cancer-free year. Another simply praised God for his faithfulness concerning a family situation. The atmosphere was electric. We sat in what felt like a holy awe, waiting, anticipating what was going to happen next.

What surprised me the most were the nationalities of those speaking. The church I attend is predominantly white and middle class. Of the eight people who testified, three were African American, one was Israeli, another was Haitian, and the remaining three were Caucasian. This time for testifying provided space for the marginalized in our midst to be heard, giving the congregation the opportunity to listen to voices we might otherwise not have.

This time for testifying provided space for the marginalized in our midst to be heard, giving the congregation the opportunity to listen to voices we might otherwise not have.

Despite their familiarity with the practice of testifying, none of the teenagers stood to speak. I was not disappointed. Instead, I was overwhelmed with gratitude that the teenagers to my right and to my left were being exposed to the spiritual narratives of those both older and different from them, to a language in which many of us long to be proficient.

It is good for Christians to testify. It is edifying for Christians to testify. It is also very dangerous for Christians to testify. If the great theologian Karl Barth admits his inability to speak of God, what of the laity? What of *adolescent* laity? With testimony comes a potentially dangerous shift of power. The clergy are no longer the only ones speaking of God; the laity is given a platform as well. Those with an ecclesial history of testifying can easily identify the dangers: testimonies that drag on in such a way that the congregation gets another sermon; testimonies that are repeated week after week, word for word, leaving the congregation not with a new word of edification but with an old, worn-out story that functions as a kind of sentimental liturgy; and testimonies that highlight the speaker as opposed to God. Perhaps most dangerous of all are the testimonies that attribute things to God that ought *not* be attributed to God, leaving the congregation with harmful theological assertions that must be cleaned up later by the pastor. Allowing the laity, regardless of their age, to speak of God is both empowering and dangerous.

Pastor Lillian Daniel of First Congregational Church in Glen Ellyn, Illinois, recounts a breakfast meeting with a fellow pastor in her town, "a charismatic and evangelical church pastor." Daniel was considering introducing the practice of testifying to her congregation as a form of Lenten reflection and she shared her intentions with her colleague. "Why on earth do you want to do that?" the charismatic pastor asked. "If there was one thing I wish I could get rid of in my service, it would be those testimonies!" This pastor went on to explain how "in her Spirit-filled church, the service began with lengthy spontaneous sharing of testimonies offered by whoever felt moved. 'You know how it is,' she said. 'It's the same people getting up every time, using it as a chance to be in the spotlight, taking things over.'"[1]

It is good for Christians to testify. It is edifying for Christians to testify. It is also very dangerous for Christians to testify.

This openness has the potential to threaten the established clerical system. Scholars such as Christian Collins Winn and Donald Dayton have identified testimony as a practice for the marginalized.[2] Throughout history we see evidence of women and minorities and those on the margins being empowered in places where testimonies of the laity were both allowed and encouraged. This kind of theological leveling of the playing field pulled those who might otherwise have been considered on the margins of religious life to the center, giving them a voice and allowing them to speak of God.

Throughout history we see evidence of women and minorities and those on the margins being empowered in places where testimonies of the laity were both allowed and encouraged.

We saw a similar shift of power when the Bible became available in the vernacular. For centuries, medieval Christianity of the West heard the Scriptures read aloud in Latin, with objections to vernacular language widely documented.[3] Those reading the Bible without

---

[1] Lillian Daniel, *Tell It Like It Is: Reclaiming the Practice of Testimony* (Herndon, VA: Alban Institute, 2006), p. xiii.

[2] Christian T. Collins Winn, ed., *From the Margins: A Celebration of the Theological Work of Donald W. Dayton* (Eugene, OR: Pickwick, 2007). See especially the essays "Piety and Radicalism: Ante-Bellum Social Evangelicalism in the U.S.," pp. 31-42 and "'Good News to the Poor': The Methodist Experience After Wesley," pp. 77-108.

[3] Pope Innocent III warned against Scripture in the vernacular: "Usually [the mysteries of faith] cannot be understood by everyone but only by those who are qualified to understand them with

an episcopal license were in danger of making grave errors of interpretation. Scriptures in the vernacular, combined with the Gutenberg press, proved dangerous for the church as Martin Luther articulated an understanding of the priesthood of all believers. Just as an accessible Bible was empowering to the laity, so is allowing the laity to testify. With the Reformation and the Counter-Reformation came a growing appreciation for the formative value of the Scripture in the vernacular.

To say that we believe it possible for laity—even *adolescent* laity—to testify to the triune God does not mean that just anyone can stand up at any time and say anything. A priesthood of all believers does not give carte blanche to any kind of testimony. Just as the legal system offers guidelines on what constitutes a properly ordered testimony, so the church can and should explore and adhere to a responsible practice of testimony. Within the remainder of this chapter I will present a series of guidelines for a responsible practice of adolescent testimony. These guidelines will revolve around the ideas of (1) seeing, (2) hearing and (3) speaking. Before students can testify, they must *see* where God is at work. In addition to seeing, their *ears* must be exposed to the language of testimony. Then, when they have the eyes to see and the ears to hear, they are in a better position to *articulate* a responsible testimony themselves.

The eyes, the ears and the mouths to speak will take on a concrete form as I highlight the youth group of College Wesleyan Church in central Indiana. This youth group is committed to exercising a responsible practice of testifying. Interviews with this church provide us a picture of what testifying at its finest might look like. Of course, every practice carries with it potential baggage, and testifying is no different. Using College Wesleyan's youth group as an exemplar, we will explore the difficulties this youth group has encountered as well as the dangers they navigated in making the practice of testifying an integral part of their worship experience in a responsible and edifying manner.

---

informed intelligence. The depth of the divine Scriptures is such that not only the illiterate and uninitiated have difficulty understanding them, but also the educated and the gifted" (Peter Hünermann, Helmut Hoping, Robert L. Fastiggi, Anne E. Nash and Heinrich Denzinger, *Enchiridion Symbolorum: Compendium of Creeds, Definitions, and Declarations on Matters of Faith and Morals* [San Francisco: Ignatius, 2012], pp. 770-71).

Eyes to See: Cultivating Hopeful Expectation for God's Presence in Our World

John and I had been married for almost five years when we found out we were expecting our first child. Instantly our perspectives changed. I remember walking around the mall with my husband, his wide eyes frantically moving back and forth along the aisles. Finally he blurted out in disbelief, "There are kids everywhere!" Now, there was nothing unusual about this trip to the mall. We had walked this mall countless

> **In order for teenagers to testify to God's presence in their lives they must first be *aware* of God's presence in their lives.**

times before. There was also not an unusual infestation of children on this particular occasion. But we were different. We were expecting our first child, and we saw children *everywhere*. This awareness of the child I was carrying prompted an awareness of other children. Nothing about the situation had changed, but our perspectives had.

God continually manifests himself in our lives. We, however, are not always aware of these holy manifestations. In order for teenagers to testify to God's presence in their lives they must first be *aware* of God's presence in their lives. They must have the eyes to see. Here I am referring to living in a state of perpetual advent—always waiting, looking and hoping for the presence of God. Indeed, advent is more than simply waiting; the term implies a rich, cultivated hope that God is active and moving in our world. Perpetual advent means we are always seeking out and hoping for the sanctifying presence of God. God is active in our world. What is more, God's activity in this world is available to us and forms us further into the image of Christ, altering our minds and our actions so that the children of God more and more begin to resemble our heavenly Father. This idea of perpetual advent is not to suggest that there are times when God is not present, only that there are

> **Advent is more than simply waiting; the term implies a rich, cultivated hope that God is active and moving in our world. Perpetual advent means we are always seeking out and hoping for the sanctifying presence of God.**

times in our lives when we seem to be more aware of or susceptible to God's presence.

Generally speaking, my hunch is that adolescents tend to live in Advent-like states during the highly concentrated times that come at camp and in missions trip environments.[4] Many teenagers and youth pastors alike expect, or at least *hope*, that some kind of experience with God will manifest itself. In fact, if churches do make space for adolescents to testify, it is often after these kinds of experiences. It is not uncommon, at least in evangelical churches, for teenagers to return from a trip and testify to their

> **But what if teenagers returned home from their missions trip with the expectation that God might still be at work in their life? What if teenagers left youth camp with the hope that they might still encounter the presence of God in their hometown?**

experiences of building homes in Mexico or their week away at camp. I certainly applaud the space made for this kind of testifying to take place. My concern, however, is that if camps and missions trips are the *only* times testimonies are called for, the implicit message given is that these "disorienting dilemmas" are the only times in which God breaks into our world. Adolescents often expect God to be present in their lives on a missions trip or at camp, and youth pastors often instruct their teenagers to be on the lookout for God during these experiences. Often, in evangelical settings, both teenagers and youth pastors approach trips and camps with an advent perspective, expecting God to be at work. They are more susceptible to what some might call God-sightings.

But what if teenagers returned home from their missions trip with the expectation that God might still be at work in their lives? What if teenagers left youth camp with the hope that they might still encounter the presence of God in their hometown? If we want teenagers to keep this Advent-like state in their day-to-day lives, we must live in the conviction that God is regularly breaking into our lives and in our normal, everyday routines. This means we create space for testifying after camp as well as on a Wednesday evening in the middle of March. I am not suggesting

---

[4]Jack Mezirow refers to these times as "disorienting dilemmas"; see *Transformative Dimensions of Adult Learning* (San Francisco: Jossey-Bass, 1991), p. 167.

that we deny the uniqueness of disorienting dilemmas; rather, I'm suggesting that we take seriously the time we have with our teenagers regardless of whether we are in Mexico or simply attending weekly youth group. God is as active at home as he is at youth camp, and we can give space to hear about it on a regular basis. When we model to our teenagers our assumption that God is active within his children's lives, we help form within them a kind of hopeful expectation that provides them with the eyes to see God's work.

I am not suggesting that we are the ones who *create* God's presence; rather, we are witnesses to God's presence and invite others to look with us. We do not cause God's in-breaking; we call *attention* to God's in-breaking.

Let me be clear: I am not suggesting that we are the ones who *create* God's presence; rather, we are witnesses to God's presence and invite others to look with us. We do not cause God's in-breaking; we call *attention* to God's in-breaking. We do not create the divine; we try to help form our teenagers to know how to see and respond to the divine.

Oliver Sacks, professor of neurology and psychiatry at Columbia University Medical Center, provides a helpful image for youth pastors in understanding their role in the spiritual formation of teenagers. Sacks's work was exhibited in the 1998 film *At First Sight* and provides insights into the restoration of sight.[5] In the film, the character Virgil undergoes an experimental surgery that restores the sight he lost as an infant. As the doctor removes the bandages from his eyes, Virgil cries, "Something's wrong. . . . It's all screwed up. This can't be seeing. Something's wrong." Although Virgil's eyes have physically been repaired, his mind is not yet able to process this new visual information. Virgil's doctor attempts to explain this to him:

> Ok, Virgil. Says here you went blind at one, before you developed a visual vocabulary. You have no sense of depth of field, no knowledge of space, shape, size or distance. Basically your eyes work but your brain hasn't learned to process the information. You are mentally blind. Neurologists call this "visual agnosia."[6]

[5]*At First Sight* was based on Sacks's essay "To See and Not See" from his book *An Anthropologist on Mars: Seven Paradoxical Tales* (New York: Knopf, 1995), pp. 107-52.
[6]*At First Sight*, dir. Irwin Winkler (Hollywood, CA: Metro-Goldwyn-Mayer, 1999).

Sacks explains that Virgil would often become startled by his own shadow: "(the whole concept of shadows, of objects blocking light was puzzling to him) and [he] would come to a stop, or trip, or try to step over it."[7] Sacks further explains Virgil's situation, reflecting:

> The rest of us, born sighted, can scarcely imagine such confusion. For we, born with a full complement of senses, and correlating these, one with the other, create a sight world from the start, a work of visual objects and concepts and meanings. When we open our eyes each morning, it is upon a world we have spent a lifetime *learning* to see. We are not given the world: we make our world through incessant experience, categorization, memory, reconnection.[8]

Virgil's experience was further confused by well-meaning family members who still treated him as if he were blind: "his seeing identity [was] denied or undermined, and he responded, compliantly, by acting, or even becoming blind—a massive withdrawal or regression of part of his ego to a crushing annihilating denial of identity."[9] Virgil's ability to navigate as a seeing man in a seeing world was dependent not only on his reintegrating his sight with his other senses but also having supportive people around him helping him explore and live into this new identity.

Youth pastors have the privilege of coming alongside both the seeing and the blind as witnesses to the truth and life of Jesus Christ as well as to how the life of Jesus intersects our lives today. Youth pastors are not the ones restoring sight. They are not the ones working a miracle; rather, youth pastors come alongside teenagers and attempt to help them see. Depth perception, color, shadow—all of these factors play into the art of seeing. Youth pastors do not and cannot force the presence of God. They can, however, help train the eyes of teenagers to be aware of God's presence. What's more, they can help our teenagers live into these fluctuating identities by encouraging them to keep practicing living as "seeing" people. Before we can ask teenagers to testify, they must be able to see the presence of God. This does not mean they will have a fully articulate understanding of this experience, only that they might have enough guidance to at least gesture toward where they

---

[7]Sacks, "To See and Not See," p. 120.
[8]Ibid., p. 114.
[9]Ibid., p. 137.

see God at work in such a way that the community is then in a position to help fill in the blanks.

Youth pastors can also help teenagers see where God might be at work in their lives by sanctifying the mundane. Youth groups often allow for weekly share times of "highs and lows" or "roses and thorns," where each teenager shares a highlight and a lowlight from the week before. We can help train their eyesight by slightly shifting our questions and sanctifying what is often seen as simply mundane: "Where might God have been present in the normal, ordinary parts of your day?" we might ask, giving teenagers an opportunity to reinterpret anything they might have assumed was coincidence. Asking this question regularly may help create a hopeful expectation that Jesus Christ can and does move in everyday life. What we are doing is teaching our teenagers to look at their lives anew with a spiritual lens. We attempt to limit assertions of coincidence or happenstance and instead see God as the author of life and the giver of good and perfect gifts.

Those who have seen the Disney movie *Pinocchio* will be familiar with the character Jiminy Cricket and his tagline to "always let your conscience be your guide." Young people often hear their consciences referred to when trying to discern right from wrong. What if the church took that which most teenagers already assume—some idea of a conscience that helps discern good choices—and suggested that what steers us toward what is good and right could actually be the voice of God? Cultivating a sense of hopeful expectation may mean reframing what is already taken for granted in the understanding that God is already actively present in our lives.

We must help teenagers live in a state of advent to *expect* God to be present in their lives and resist any urge to find luck as the author of their fate. I imagine this could raise a number of questions in some people's minds: But surely you are not suggesting that God is always able to be seen in our lives. What about those times when God's absence is palpably seen? What of the saints who throughout the centuries reported feeling an absence of God? What of Jesus' cry of abandonment in the moments prior to his death? How can we tell our teenagers to expect the presence of God when centuries of Christians have reported different experiences?

Those Christians who speak of sensing the absence of God only voice such convictions after having experienced the presence of God. You are not aware of God's absence until you are aware of God's presence. Those within the intertestamental period who longed for the coming of the Messiah yet did not live long enough to witness the incarnation did not waste their lives in waiting. That time of expectation was still time well spent. Those who are not actively seeing the presence of God may be in more need of hearing testimonies than the rest of us. We see the heartfelt benefits of a vicarious faith where, though I might not be able to sense the presence of God in my life at present, I am hearing about the ways in which God is active in my friend's life, which might give me hope that God is indeed real and cares about the lives of his children.

Of course, there is the danger that people who do not sense the presence of God may be frustrated or saddened at the thought of God being present to someone else and absent to themselves. I remember David, a fifteen-year-old boy, coming to me at the end of a youth retreat expressing sorrow that he just did not "feel God" the way other kids in the youth group claimed to feel God.[10] I wish I had a better answer for him than what I offered at the time. I said something about patience and continued openness for the presence of God, but I wish I had been more present with him in his sorrow and helped him explore what it was he was wanting from God. Did he simply want the emotional high his friends seemed to be experiencing? Was he searching for reassurance that God was real? Was there a specific area in his life where he needed divine intervention? When we speak of positioning our teenagers in an Advent-like state, the hope is that they will be given eyes to see God at work and testify to that effect. But the truth of the matter is, even if they are unable to sense the presence of God, the desire for God is still commendable. David may not have been able to articulate any kind of awareness of God's presence, but the truth of the matter was, he *was* talking about God. Implicit within his words was a desire to feel close with God, to experience some kind of "personal liberation," to use Barth's words. Though David was not sensing the presence of God like his friends were, he was still

---

[10]Name has been changed.

being exposed to the idea of a rich and full Christian life. Even articulation of God's absence is an opportunity to practice God talk.

For those having difficulty sensing God's presence, hearing testimonies about others' difficulty in sensing God might be extremely helpful. I imagine David would have greatly appreciated hearing a testimony from someone who confessed to feeling absent from God for a period of her life. David might have found great hope in solidarity in hearing from a Christian who did not sense he was "experiencing God" for a period of his life. Too often, testimonies are touted as spiritual success stories. A mature spirituality acknowledges the waxing and waning that comes with long-term Christian living.

> **Too often, testimonies are touted as spiritual success stories. A mature spirituality acknowledges the waxing and waning that comes with long-term Christian living.**

What of those teenagers who grew up in secular settings where even the name of God is a foreign concept? What of those who find it difficult to express their emotions or are just shy in general?

In some ways, the idea of testifying might come more easily to those who have grown up hearing regular God-talk and who find it easy to access and express their emotions. Testifying, however, is not limited to one demographic or personality type. We give teenagers a great gift when we expose them to a wide range of testimonies. They are at an advantage when they hear that the even-keeled, methodical outline of a narrative from William is just as valid and worthy of hearing as the bubbly, emotional testimony of Janelle. Lillian Daniel, the Congregationalist pastor who ushered in the practice of testifying to her mainline church, addresses the misconception that testifying is for the extroverted who find it easy to relay their feelings: "Not all our testimonies at church in New Haven were emotional," she writes, "but most were. People who in normal conversation might be described as reserved or even aloof revealed a depth of feeling in their testimonies that took us by surprise. It was not so much the display of emotion, or dramatic presentation or reading, but more the depth of emotion in the words chosen."[11]

---

[11]Daniel, *Tell It Like It Is*, p. xxii.

Adam McHugh, author of *Introverts in the Church: Finding Our Place in an Extroverted Culture*, encourages churches to help create more comfortable environments "and contexts that feel natural" to introverts.[12] In the case of testifying this might mean allowing for more planned testimonies that don't rely on spontaneity. We can seek out written testimonies in advance or allow for more informal, small group or one-on-one opportunities to share.

When the church is exposed to the narratives of extroverted and introverted alike, that exposure in itself is a form of testimony stating that God is just as present in one personality type as God is in others. McHugh explains: "Introverted seekers need introverted evangelists. . . . Introverted seekers need to know and see that it's possible to lead the Christian life as themselves. It's imperative for them to understand that becoming a Christian is not tantamount with becoming an extrovert."[13]

Teaching teenagers how to look for God, training their eyes to perceive the spiritual shadows and gradations of color and depth, means that we are continually looking for God, whether in a kind of radical in-breaking or through the sanctifying of the mundane or in that which we might otherwise write off as coincidence. It also means acknowledging God's otherness and transcendence. As a free agent, God cannot be forced to appear by any kind of formulation on our part. God is free to manifest himself or hide himself. Our job is to simply keep our eyes open for God's coming.

EARS TO HEAR: ACQUIRING THE LANGUAGE TO TESTIFY

Those interested in encouraging teenagers to testify may be tempted to create some kind of curriculum or training program on how to testify. Well-meaning youth leaders may be tempted to formally introduce teenagers to proper talk of God. Before much effort is spent on formal, educational scope and sequence programs, however, it is helpful to take into account the following factors: First, the average seventh grader picks up

---

[12]Adam McHugh, *Introverts in the Church: Finding Our Place in an Extroverted Culture* (Downers Grove, IL: InterVarsity Press, 2009), p. 178.

[13]Ibid., pp. 184-85. For more on this topic, please see Madie's story on page 163.

between ten and fifteen new words a day.[14] Second, fewer than one of these words is acquired through formal educational methods. The vast majority of these words are picked up by other means. They may have been acquired through reading the word used in context or hearing the word being spoken and teasing the meaning out of its surrounding context. This is roughly known as "latent semantic analysis" (LSA). The simplified thesis of LSA is that the majority of the language we acquire does not come about through intentional instruction but is picked up in context while the word is simply being used in everyday life. Proponents of LSA would state that within each individual lies the capacity to figure out more words and their meanings in informal settings. What we learn from LSA is that if we want our teenagers to acquire certain language about God, this acquisition most naturally takes place in more organic, informal experiences.

> **The average seventh grader picks up between ten and fifteen new words a day. Fewer than one of these words is acquired through formal educational methods. The vast majority of these words are picked up by other means.**

Of course, this idea may be intuitive for some. It is not disputed that language acquisition tends to occur more fully in immersion experiences as opposed to formal times of teaching. So the man who travels to Germany finds that his ability to speak the language skyrockets in his three months abroad as opposed to the three years of daily study in a school.

I took high school French when I was a teenager. I was a good student—I studied, I memorized phrases, I made good grades. When my husband and I visited France on our honeymoon, I was able to pose my questions with great fluency: "*Où se trouve un hôtel?*" My question concerning the location of a hotel, however, was met with a rapid response I was unable to interpret. I knew stock phrases in the French language, but I was unable to play with the language.

Along similar lines, as much as I would love for my children to be able

---

[14]Thomas K. Landauer and Susan T. Dumais, "A Solution to Plato's Problem: The Latent Semantic Analysis Theory of Acquisition, Induction, and Representation of Knowledge," *Psychological Review* 104, no. 2 (1997): 211-40. For further reading, see Thomas K. Landauer, *Handbook of Latent Semantic Analysis* (Mahwah, NJ: Lawrence Erlbaum Associates, 2007).

to recite the Westminster Confession of Faith, I'm less concerned with whether or not they can give the Sunday school stock phrase answer. I want to see them able to *play* with their religious language. I want them to be able to say, "Give us this day our daily bread," but I also want them to be able to articulate a time in which the Lord provided that bread. To draw from a musical analogy, it's almost as if the creeds and catechisms are theory work or scales. This kind of knowledge grounds us in a particular context. If the Apostles' Creed is the scales, then the testimony is the sonata where we can play with the music. The creeds ground us theologically and the testimony allows us to play within these bounds.

If we want our teenagers to be able to articulate where they understand God to be at work in their lives, we must immerse them in God talk. The best way to share language is not necessarily in formal settings of instruction but through immersion—allowing them to hear others' stories. First we encourage an Advent-like expectation and then we expose them to regular, organic talk of God.

> I want them to be able to say, "Give us this day our daily bread," but I also want them to be able to articulate a time in which the Lord provided that bread. To draw from a musical analogy, it's almost as if the creeds and catechisms are theory work or scales. This kind of knowledge grounds us in a particular context. If the Apostles' Creed is the scales, then the testimony is the sonata where we can play with the music. The creeds ground us theologically and the testimony allows us to play within these bounds.

When we expose our teenagers to God talk we are doing more than telling them stories. We are constructing identities. Our words help create their present "reality." Our language does more than describe events; we are offering firmer contours to belief. Teenagers *will* talk. Teenagers will have a repertoire of topics they can adequately articulate. The question we are faced with is, what kind of language will our teenagers use?

We expose our teenagers to spiritual narratives not for entertainment value and not just to engage their imaginations. Rather, we expose them to spiritual narratives because the Holy Spirit uses our narratives to construct spiritual identities. We expose our teenagers to spiritual narratives because we recognize, along with Jeffrey Stout, that our dearest life commitments are often embedded in these stories.[15] We immerse our teenagers in these stories hoping that they will take on this "accent" to which they are exposed.

What does language immersion look like when it concerns teenagers? It means that we expose them to the testimonies of people of all ages. When I speak of language acquisition I do not necessarily mean teaching teenagers new theological terms like *justification* or *docetism*; rather, I am referring to exposing teenagers to a *kind* of talk—almost an accent or a dialect to what they already use.

I remember participating in a middle school missions trip to New Orleans where our northern teenagers were struck by the drawls and long *i* sounds that permeated the speech of the local inhabitants. By the end of the week everyone was practicing their drawls. A few students insisted that they had actually acquired an accent without even trying. No one sat down and informed the teenagers how to draw out a word, adding syllables along the way; this simple experience of immersion was enough to affect the way they spoke. When we are immersed in a situation that elevates a certain kind of speech, it is very difficult to not pick up that to which we are exposed.

When my son Sam was three years old he surprised me with his theological acquisition of language. As I was putting him to bed Sam informed me that God had healed his sick kitty. The thing was, Sam did not have a kitty. Not a real one at least. Instead, he held up a ratty stuffed animal and said, "God healed kitty. Now her owie is smaller than a dust mite" (apparently Sam had also acquired language in relation to his severe allergies). I do not recall intentional conversations with Sam about praying for healing, but somehow he picked up on this concept through everyday conversations in our home. Sam was practicing his God talk. In this particular case, Sam was not necessarily tapping into some deep, theological truth. Did God heal a stuffed animal? Well no, not really. But rather than correct my child's overactive imagination I decided to play with him in hopes of honing this Advent-like hope. "Oh he did?" I responded. "Well if God healed kitty, what should you say to God?" I asked. "Thank you," Sam said firmly.

---

[15]Jeffrey Stout, "Liberal Society and the Language of Morals," *Soundings* 69 (1986): 37.

Sam's crediting God for healing his stuffed animal is somewhat silly and certainly not edifying in itself, but it was a time for Sam to practice talking of God as well as practicing how to respond to God when he senses God is at work. God moves and we respond with gratitude. Sam's ears were in the process of being trained as he acquired new ways of talking of God.[16]

I should highlight at this point that while I was exposed to testimonies as a child in a formal worship setting, this kind of God talk was also prevalent in my home. Talk of God was assumed. My parents looked for God throughout their everyday lives in the same way one might expect to run into an old friend in her hometown. You could say talk of God was my native tongue just as much as English. This kind of exposure, Christian Smith and Melissa Denton would say, is ideal as we acquire a greater capacity to speak when we are regularly exposed to native speakers of the tongue we are trying to acquire.

The infusion of religious language through narratives is a great gift the church can give its congregants. When this language is also spoken at home, both in organic conversations in the minivan as well as during intentional times around the dinner table, there is a kind of language facility that is undeniable. Of course, that is not to say that all talk of God at home or church is positive. No doubt there have been abuses of God's name, which can make testifying both frightening and dangerous.

Taking Barth's warnings into account regarding being simultaneously unable to speak and compelled to speak of God, teenagers should be exposed to clear yet circumspect language of God. The kind of language teenagers encounter should be full of discernment. Recognizing that there is a large margin for error in both reporting and interpreting what one thinks is an encounter with God, we would be wise to expose our teenagers to tempered phrases such as "I could be wrong, but . . ." and, "I think I am led to . . ." This kind of language leaves room for the body of Christ to help interpret one's experience and models humility, which opens the door for teenagers to share an experience they are unsure of. The message being sent is, "If you are unsure about something that you

---

[16]Of course, there is God talk that needs to be corrected, which will be addressed shortly.

have experienced, feel free to bring it to the church for interpretation." This may sound like an encouragement toward using disclaimers or defensive statements. What we are trying to cultivate, however, is an articulate discernment or wisdom. This kind of tempered language nods toward the transcendence of God with the acknowledgment that we are unable to fully comprehend the movement of God.

In addition to language of discernment, it is helpful to immerse students in honest, transparent language where the "curtain is pulled back," meaning the people testifying might admit to feeling anxious about public speaking; or perhaps the speakers testify that they somehow feel compelled to share what they are about to say. There is no reason to think that testimonies should only be given by the confident and sure. In fact, it could be beneficial to be honest concerning our fears and anxiety connected not only with public speaking in general but also with public speaking concerning an all-powerful God.

Recognizing that there is a large margin for error in both reporting and interpreting what one thinks is an encounter with God, we would be wise to expose our teenagers to tempered phrases such as "I could be wrong, but . . ." and, "I think I am led to . . ." This kind of language leaves room for the body of Christ to help interpret one's experience.

Some might wonder just who is supposed to be testifying during this period of language acquisition. Who should be exhibiting this God talk? In addition to giving teenagers the opportunity to testify, we would be wise to widen the testimonial circle to include any adult leaders working alongside the teenagers—the adults whom the teenagers (hopefully) already trust and have a relationship with. While the testimony of an elderly church member or a former youth group member may be helpful, there is something very special about hearing one's normal acquaintances be vocal on this matter.

No doubt this will make some adult leaders very uncomfortable, causing them to ask, "How am I supposed to talk about something that is so transcendent? How can I speak of something so other?" We actually do this all the time. Many of us have no problem speaking of the mind-boggling (outer space), the fantastical (a trip to Bora Bora) or the absurd (fairy tales). While I do not want to compare Jesus to the tooth fairy, I do want to stress how often it is that we talk about things that are beyond our comprehension. What is more, when we share our testimony, we are not just talking about a dead or distant subject; we are talking about a living God who reveals himself over and over again. And we are not speaking by ourselves; we speak with the empowerment of the Holy Spirit. The faint of heart might also appreciate the reminder that we are not asking for a homily or a theological treatise of one's experience. We are simply looking for a narration of something that happened.

Then, of course, there are those who might say, "I prefer to keep my faith private. I do not want my spiritual experiences to influence the teens in my care. I want them to decide for themselves." By not talking about your faith, you are not remaining a neutral presence. Drawing on theories of social reality mentioned in chapter two, silence can actually invalidate the plausibility of faith. By not talking about your faith you are not giving your teenagers options; you are actually taking options away.

But how can a teenager discern whether or not what they are experiencing is from God or from something else? How will teenagers be able to recognize what they see as truly being of God? Perhaps one of the most helpful ways in discerning how to see God today involves looking at how God has moved in the past. Nehemiah's story about rebuilding the wall of Jerusalem is more than a story; it is a testimony. When Paul speaks of his experience on the Damascus road, he is not just telling a story; he is testifying. When we highlight the testimonial nature of the gospel and help teenagers see people in the Bible as average people with extraordinary in-breakings of God, we expose our teenagers to the ways in which God has moved in the past. Teenagers today are better able to recognize God's presence when they have been exposed to God's presence in a narrative format beforehand.

> When we highlight the testimonial nature of the gospel and help teenagers see people in the Bible as average people with extraordinary in-breakings of God, we expose our teenagers to the ways in which God has moved in the past. Teenagers today are better able to recognize God's presence when they have been exposed to God's presence in a narrative format beforehand.

Again, this advice is not a guarantee for increasing faith. Faith is first and foremost a gift from God. My hope, though, is that by providing teenagers with a faith language, Christian faith is seen as a valid option—something to consider. When teenagers live in an Advent-like state, hoping to see God, and when they are regularly exposed to others talking of God, they are in a better position to speak of God themselves. True God talk helps construct legitimating structures, which allow us to see and claim faith in ways we cannot by ourselves. Testimony is a way in which the Holy Spirit confirms we are God's children. Testifying is what we do out of gratitude to the triune God.

A Mouth to Speak: Incorporating the Practice of Testimony

Perhaps the most important piece in giving teenagers a mouth to speak is giving them a stage from which to speak—to provide time and space for teenagers to practice and play around with newly acquired language. Smith and Denton's suspicions with the NSYR's inarticulate teenagers are that this was the first time any of these teenagers had been asked about their faith. No one had invited them to put their spiritual journeys into words. They might have experienced encounters with God, but they were not articulated. And borrowing once again from Berger and Luckmann, "the subjective reality of something that is never talked about becomes shaky."[17]

Ammerman and James K. A. Smith could be correct that inarticulate teenagers could very well have a true, implicit Christian faith made up of "fragments" and "subplots" of their lives.[18] One can experience the presence of God without articulating the identity of that presence. But if teenagers are never given space to articulate or even gesture toward these fragments and side plots, these potentially formative experiences dim and fade at best, and at worst are misinterpreted and damaging as they replay privately in the mind of the individual teenager. Conversion experiences are common. Berger and Luckmann remind us that the chal-

---

[17]Peter L. Berger and Thomas Luckmann, *The Social Construction of Reality: A Treatise in the Sociology of Knowledge* (Garden City, NY: Doubleday, 1966), p. 52.

[18]Nancy Ammerman, *Everyday Religion: Observing Modern Religious Lives* (Oxford: Oxford University Press, 2007), p. 226. James K. A. Smith makes similar statements in *Desiring the Kingdom: Worship, Worldview, and Cultural Formation* (Grand Rapids: Baker Academic, 2009), p. 43.

lenge is to continue to live into this conversion within the community. But how can this be done? If the professionals of the NSYR could not get teenagers to access latent stories or beliefs, how might untrained youth leaders ignite this practice within their own churches?

The truth of the matter is, those who desire to cultivate a practice of testimony within their ministries will find that they seldom are "starting from scratch." Many youth groups have testimonial "loopholes" that are already a part of their program and simply need to be cultivated and nurtured. And many of the practices that take place within the church in general are directly or indirectly related to the practice of testimony.[19]

The truth of the matter is, those who desire to cultivate a practice of testimony within their ministries will find that they seldom are "starting from scratch." Many youth groups have testimonial "loopholes" that are already a part of their program and simply need to be cultivated and nurtured.

As can be seen in figure 5.1, testimony often serves as a function of other practices. Though a church might not see themselves as engaging in the practice of testimony, many will see overlap with testimony in the practices in which they already engage. Most will find that they are not necessarily starting something new when introducing the concept of testifying; they can, in fact, simply adapt

---

[19]Here I am referring to Alasdair MacIntyre's definition of "practice" as "any coherent and complex form of socially established co-operative human activity through which goods internal to that form of activity are realised in the course of trying to achieve those standards of excellence which are appropriate to, and partially definitive of, that form of activity, with the result that human powers to achieve excellence, and human conceptions of the ends and goods involved, are systematically extended" (*After Virtue: A Study in Moral Theory* [Notre Dame, IN: University of Notre Dame Press, 2007], p. 187). These practices involve "standards of excellence and obedience to rules as well as achievement of goods. To enter into a practice is to accept the authority of those standards and the inadequacy of my own performance as judged by them" (ibid., p. 190). Craig Dykstra offers a helpful description of practice as "participation in a cooperatively formed pattern of activity that emerges out of a complex tradition of interactions among many people sustained over a long period of time" (Craig Dykstra, "Reconceiving Practice in Theological Inquiry and Education," in *Virtues and Practices in the Christian Tradition*, ed. Nancey Murphy, Brad Kallenbery and Mark Thiessen Nation [Harrisburg, PA: Trinity Press International, 1997], p. 170). He corrects the misunderstanding of seeing a practice as an individualistic, ahistorical act by directing us to Jeffrey Stout's understanding of practice as being comparable to a game of baseball. It cannot be played alone. "It is fundamentally cooperative. If you can't get a team together you can't play the game" (Jeffrey Stout, *Ethics After Babel: The Languages of Morals and Their Discontents* [Boston: Beacon, 1988], p. 276; see also p. 303). This is an important concept to grasp—testimonies are not an individual act but a communal practice where a testimony is *shared* and the congregation responds with affirmation or a challenge.

practices that are already taking place. A youth group that regularly takes prayer requests from teenagers is well poised to organically introduce the idea of testimony. When a fourteen-year-old boy asks for prayer for his mother who is looking for a job, the youth leader can give space for this boy to report on whether or not the prayer has been answered. If, in fact, the boy's mother finds a job, the youth leader might gently press to see if there is a story behind this answer to prayer. How did this answer to prayer come about? Where might God have been involved in her acquiring this job? Even if a clear answer to prayer is not seen, calling upon the narrative

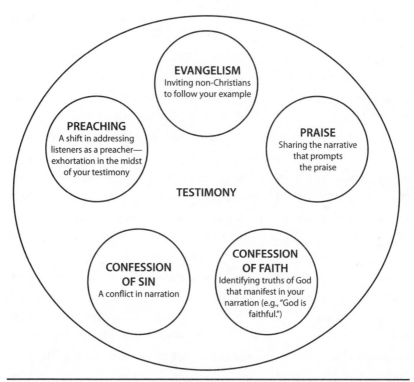

Figure 5.1. Testimony as a function of other practices: how and where testimony shows up in other practices related to testifying. *(Here I am bringing the practice of testimony in conversation with other practices of the church that often overlap with testifying. I am not addressing an exhaustive list of church practices by any means, only those which are pertinent to the discussion.)*

element of the request is a kind of testimony that at the very least increases ease in talking about God and prompts the teenager to an Advent-like state.

If a youth group regularly draws from liturgy or some kind of call to worship, the youth leader might ask a question following the reading to the effect of, "Has someone seen God as 'mighty to save' this week?"

Perhaps the most common way in which testimonies stealthily enter our churches is in the form of sermon illustrations. Here youth leaders might speak about an experience with God that led them to a certain understanding or decision. For example, when they draw from a psalm of lament, they might identify a time in their life when it seemed as if God had "forgotten to be gracious" or "slammed the door on his compassion" (Ps 77:9 NLT).

The point is, testifying is almost a practice churches can "lean into." Parents and youth workers alike can begin by asking simple questions in everyday conversations. We can identify those times in which we have sensed God breaking into our own lives. Incorporating this practice means taking a critical look at whatever practices we already have in place and asking ourselves poignant questions about the relationships between what we are already doing and what we hope to be doing.

Much of what I have been sharing up to this point is most suited for an evangelical context. However, I do not mean to limit this practice to evangelical settings (though that is my background). Pastor Lillian Daniel speaks of her own journey of bringing this "evangelical" concept into her mainline setting. Describing the testimony services she heard in more evangelical settings, Daniel admits testimonies of "ecstatic praise, claiming Jesus as Lord and Savior" would not be comfortable expressions of faith for her Congregationalist church. "But," she writes, "I also knew that we had a faith story to tell one another. Why couldn't we practice testimony too? Besides," she continues, "the practice flowed naturally out of our own congregational history, in which new members gave a seven-part conversion narrative before the whole congregation; or the days of the First and Second Great Awakenings, when laypeople were freed to proclaim their own experience of God."[20] Testimonies may be more commonly found in evangelical settings today, but as the Church of the Redeemer in New Haven, Connecticut, can attest, there is no reason why this spiritually edifying practice should remain solely on evangelical ground. When it

---

[20]Lillian Daniel, *Tell It Like It Is: Reclaiming the Practice of Testimony* (Herndon, VA: Alban Institute, 2006), p. xiv.

came to introducing testimony to her congregation, Daniel found it very natural to introduce this concept as a Lenten reflection. She admits that her hesitancy to describe this practice as testifying had much to do with the proliferation of attorneys in the congregation.[21]

One of the promptings behind Daniel's decision to introduce these "Lenten reflections" was the Sunday morning announcements. Now, Sunday morning announcements are not found on any list of practices of the church that I have come across, and yet these announcements drew Daniel's awareness to the openness and perhaps even hunger of her congregants for an opportunity to share spiritual narratives. She admits her love-hate relationship with announcements, noting that some can be long and tedious. But the more she listened to these announcements the more she heard her congregants sneaking in stories. "People were using the announcements to tell stories, to tell one another in short and perhaps flip ways about themselves and about their faith. In telling the church about the next community-organizing event, they might testify to the power of the last one and the beauty of seeing all those people of faith together."[22]

Daniel also observed testimonies popping up during times of prayer: "Prayer requests were turning into small testimonies"; the church was hearing background on prayer requests as well as narratives of prayers that were answered.[23] For three years in a row Daniel heard her congregants express eager anticipation for stewardship seasons where they might once again hear members of the church offer what they called "giving moments."[24] While no one in the congregation used the word *testimony* to describe these acts, Daniel had little doubt her congregation was, in fact, testifying. And so Daniel decided to "lean into" these practices and habits already taking place within her congregation and added a slightly more formal version, giving her congregants space behind the lectern to testify at regular intervals.

That is not to say that *all* practices have overlap with testimony. In order to understand the concept of testimony it is important to understand not

---

[21]Ibid., p. 1.
[22]Ibid., pp. 8-9.
[23]Ibid., p. 9.
[24]Ibid., p. 10.

just where testifying overlaps with practices of the church but also it is *distinct* from practices of the church. Figure 5.2 illustrates how testimony functions as a practice among other practices, or where and how testifying is distinct from other practices of the church. So even though forms of testimony often emerge within sermons where personal illustrations are told, it is not necessary for testifying to emerge within a sermon. Testimonies require a personal narrative. Sermons may contain a personal narrative element, but they do not *require* this personal narrative; in that, these practices are distinct. Similarly, a confession of faith might require some kind of personal statement or assertion, but a personal narrative does not need to be attached. Perhaps the greatest confusion emerges in the relationship between testimony and confession of sin. If an individual stands up and confesses sin, is she testifying or is she engaging in public confession?

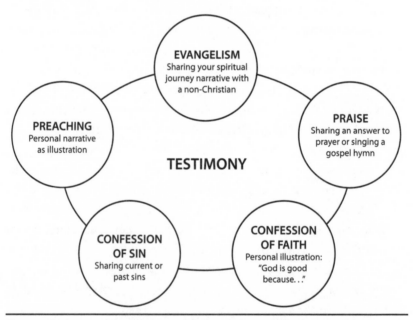

Figure 5.2. Testimony as a practice among other practices: how testifying is distinct from other practices of the church

Augustine's testimony. In order to help illustrate the distinctions between various practices of the church I will briefly draw upon Augustine's *Confessions*. While this great work is titled *Confessions*, he refers to this work as his "testimony."[25] Here already we see the importance of distinguishing testimony from other practices of the church. Here I want to pause briefly to explain the practice of confession and the practice of testimony and how they relate in the *Confessions* in order to show how Augustine's writing is in fact a testimony. I understand confession to fall under two categories: confession of faith and confession of sin. Within both categories, we see confession as being distinct from testimony and confession as a function of testimony. A confession of faith that is distinct from testimony would be a statement concerning faith that does not include a personal narrative. For example, "God is good." A confession of faith that acts as a function of testimony may be the same statement, "God is good," but there is also a narrative element: "because he provided me with a job." A confession of faith that acts as a function of testimony links a statement of faith with a personal narrative.

A confession of sin that is distinct from testimony is the act of confessing current, unforgiven sin. We see confession of sin as a function of testimony when one reports how God has forgiven one's sin. Confession of sin as a function of testimony concerns a narrative of deliverance of past sins. In this sense, if individuals speak of a sin they have already found forgiveness for, their words are a testimony to finding forgiveness. If, however, they are speaking of a current sin, they are confessing. Consider table 5.1.

Table 5.1. The Relationship Between Testimony and Confession

	Distinct from Testimony	As a Function of Testimony
Confession of Faith	"God is good."	"God is good *because* God provided me with a job."
Confession of Sin	"Forgive me for lying."	"God forgave me for lying."

Within the *Confessions*, we see many examples of confessions of faith that are distinct from the practice of testimony. We also see confessions of faith that serve as a function of testimony. For example, Augustine writes to God that he is abundantly "merciful" because God continued to hover over him even when he was immersed in sin.[26]

We do not, however, see in the *Confessions* any evidence of confession of sin that is *distinct* from testimony; we only see confession of sin as a

---

[25]Letter to Darius, in Augustine, *The Confessions and Enchiridion*, ed. Albert C. Outler (Philadelphia: Westminster Press, 1955), p. 25.

[26]Augustine, *Confessions*, 3.3.1, p. 63.

function of testimony. Augustine makes it very clear that the sins he writes of are sins for which he has already been forgiven. Jerry Root, author of *Space to Speke*, writes that we would be remiss to understand Augustine's confession to be a true confession of sin.[27] Augustine is not seeking repentance; rather, he is retelling his spiritual narrative.

Augustine's *Confessions* is considered a testimony not only because of the way he uses confession but also because of the way he uses evangelism. The *Confessions* exhibits evangelism emerging as a function of testimony. Augustine explains that he is writing for three different audiences. First, he claims, this is written "to God, but not for God," meaning he is writing to the glory of God, but God does not necessarily need these words from Augustine. And while his confession revolves around his personal narrative, he nevertheless hopes God will ultimately be glorified. In his letter to Darius he instructs him to "use [the *Confessions*] as a good man should. . . . And if something in me pleases you, here praise Him with me—Him whom I desire to be praised on my account and not myself."[28]

Table 5.2. The Relationship Between Testimony, Confession and Evangelism

	Distinct from Testimony	**As a Function of Testimony**
Confession of Faith	"God is good."	"God is good *because* God provided me with a job."
Confession of Sin	"Forgive me for lying."	"God forgave me for lying."
Evangelism	Depending on one's tradition, this may contain a "plan of salvation" that is devoid of personal narrative content. The goal is to bring another individual to a new place concerning the individual's engagement with God.*	Here someone may link a plan of salvation or an invitation to a new spiritual level with a personal narrative of his or her own spiritual journey.

*The term "plan of salvation" carries a great deal of baggage for many people; however, this is often the phrase that is used in evangelical churches where evangelism is encouraged.

Second, Augustine uses evangelism as a function of testimony to say that he is writing to fellow "sharers of mortality" and "companions of joy."[29] He hopes his words will awaken those "dozing along in despair, saying, 'I cannot,'" that they might be motivated and overjoyed at how God has

---

[27]Jerry Root, *Space to Speke: The Confessional Subject in Medieval Literature* (New York: P. Lang, 1997), pp. 15-30.
[28]Letter to Darius, in Augustine, *Confessions*, p. 25.
[29]Ibid., 10.4.6, p. 204.

helped Augustine overcome sin.[30] Ultimately he desires that his words will "excite men's minds and affections toward God."[31] Augustine admits there are voyeuristic elements to his project. Many, he writes, are simply interested in knowing about his life. Others, he writes, are more concerned with how God disciplines other people rather than how *they* might be disciplined.[32] Nevertheless, Augustine believes it necessary to write his *Confessions,* which brings us to our third point.

Augustine writes the *Confessions* for himself, in order that he might increase his love for God. He hopes that by lamenting the things of the world he might desire those things even less.[33] He also writes that he must write his *Confessions* or otherwise risk being "denied Christ in front of the holy angels."[34]

Figure 5.3. Practices as functions of testimony: how other practices emerge within the practice of testifying

[30]Ibid., 10.3.4, p. 203.
[31]"The Retractions," in Augustine, *Confessions,* p. 24.
[32]Ibid., 10.3.3, p. 202.
[33]Ibid., 10.1.1, p. 201.
[34]Ibid., 8.2.4, p. 160.

Augustine's *Confessions* is undoubtedly a testimony. It is a testimony, however, that intertwines with other practices of the church, providing us with an illustrative look at where testimony overlaps and distinguishes itself from other practices of the church.

For the sake of clarity, I should also add that many other practices often show up within the practice of testifying. Pastors who have regularly allowed for the practice of testifying within their churches will attest to the ease with which some who testify find themselves delving into other practices of the church. So it is not uncommon for a woman to stand up to testify to a particular experience and quickly transition into a quasi-sermon as she offers a challenging word to the congregation. Others might begin with a personal narrative and then make an evangelistic appeal for others to follow their example. And then there are those who end their narrative accounts with statements of belief or words of praise for that which they have received. Many churches find that testifying is often a catalyst for other practices of the church to emerge in strengthened proportions.

The nebulous nature of testifying. While the practice of testimony is distinct from other practices of the church, it is rare to hear a testimony that does not have at least some kind of overlap with other practices of the church. The figures in this chapter may appear to be nitpicky, or too technical to be of any practical use, but the practice of testifying can often take a nebulous turn. In order to practice testifying in a responsible manner it is important to understand what we mean by testimony as well as what we do not mean. Many of the pastors I spoke with on this matter were hesitant to fully embrace this practice because, in their experience, testifying meant either reciting a litany of inappropriate unconfessed sins or taking over the pulpit in order to deliver a twenty-minute sermon. *Many of the abuses that occur with the practice of testifying emerge when the lines between testifying and other practices of the church become blurry.* There are ways of clarifying these lines and keeping testimony a distinct and appropriate voice within the church, which I will explore shortly.

Once we have a clearer sense of what a testimony does and does not look like, it is helpful to understand the different kinds of testimonies as well as their settings. There are roughly two kinds of testimonies: spontaneous and ordered, and these testimonies take place in two different kinds of settings: formal and informal.

Table 5.3. Differentiating Between Kinds of Testimonies

	Spontaneous Testimony	**Ordered Testimony**
Formal Testimony	A formal, spontaneous testimony takes place when a person spontaneously decides to testify in a formal setting. For example, a pastor might invite the laity to testify in the midst of a worship service.	A formal, ordered testimony takes place when a person delivers a planned-out, perhaps written, testimony in the midst of a formal worship service.
Informal Testimony	An informal, spontaneous testimony takes place when an individual spontaneously testifies to an informally gathered group of people or to an individual outside of a formal setting.	An informal, ordered testimony takes place when one gives a previously prepared testimony to a group of people or to an individual outside of a formal setting (this might include previously prepared accounts of one's "personal liberation" or conversion story).

As illustrated in figure 5.4, there is no one way to testify. While those from a more free-church background may have strong memories of a single microphone placed on an empty stage awaiting a would-be testifier, there is nothing about that formal, spontaneous testimony that is more legitimate than the preplanned, carefully ordered testimony delivered in an informal setting.

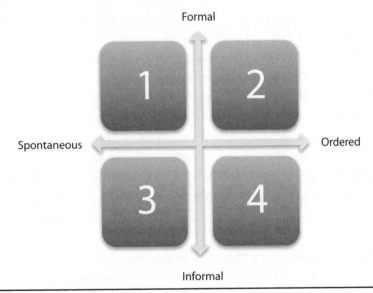

Figure 5.4. Kinds and settings of testimonies

Figure 5.4 gives plenty of room for a youth group to stretch and navigate among different kinds of testifying. Most youth groups (and most churches in general) already have at least small seeds of testifying occurring within their normal operations. Youth pastors looking to increase the practice of testimony in their church would be wise to look for places where teenagers are already talking and, as mentioned earlier, lean into these places to call out for more specific God talk.

Depending on one's youth group, certain kinds of testimonies might be easier to share than others. Those who are new to this practice might feel drawn to encourage ordered, informal testimonies. For example, teenagers might be given space at youth group to write down a simple narration of where they sense God at work. Perhaps it is as simple as filling in a blank on a sheet of paper that says, "This week I sensed God's presence when _____." Once the testimony is written down, the youth leader might then open up the floor for people to share this ordered testimony in an informal small group setting.

Likewise, if one is particularly nervous about teenagers testifying or unsure of whether or not teenagers can testify in a responsible way, he might begin by encouraging formal, ordered testimonies where a teenagers write down a testimony they would like to share in youth group at a particular time. This kind of ordered formality gives space for the youth worker to look over the testimony and ask questions or offer general feedback prior to the rest of the group receiving the testimony.

Almost all of the teenagers I interviewed claimed the only reason they testified was because their youth pastors singled them out and invited them to do so.

I should pause here and admit that in all my years in youth ministry only once have I had a teenager actually request an opportunity to testify. Most of the testimonies were invited, some even coaxed. Almost all of the teenagers I interviewed claimed the only reason they testified was because their youth pastors singled them out and invited them to do so.

Phoebe Palmer's idea of testimony involves standing up spontaneously at a testimony meeting and simply opening one's mouth, trusting that the right words will emerge. But careful thought reveals that there are multiple ways of testifying, and some may work better than others depending on the context.

College Wesleyan Church: A Look at a Responsible Practice of Testimony

While conducting interviews on teenagers and testimony, I was struck by the way in which Pastor Charlie Alcock utilized testifying with his youth group. In the middle of Indiana, at a large Wesleyan church, Charlie initiated what he called "Open House" on Sunday evenings for high school students (there was another evening designated for middle school students). From start to finish, Open House gave the appearance of being totally run by teenagers. "You will never see an adult up on stage," Charlie explains, "unless it's in a unique situation or we have one of our college students lead worship."[35] There are weekly teenage hosts welcoming and greeting the other teenagers as well as serving as emcees for the night. Teenagers play and lead worship on various instruments. But the highlight of the evening is when a teenager stands up and testifies.[36]

Charlie explains that the teenagers testifying might not realize that they are testifying. "I hardly say, 'I want you to share your testimony,'" Charlie says, "I call it, 'We just need to hear your story.'" Charlie stresses the importance of recognizing where in your story "there is an intersection of the person Jesus—where that comes to light and how their stories changed when they came to know Jesus."

Those vaguely familiar with the concept of testifying, particularly in Wesleyan circles, may have in mind a generic story of a former drug addict who was so steeped in addiction and sin before a miraculous, Damascus road transformation. Charlie speaks of addressing this sensationalism with those in his youth group: "What we're trying to teach the students here is that it doesn't have to be some terrible experience that you went through that gives you a testimony; it's simply talking

---

[35]Charlie Alcock, interview by Amanda Drury, digital recording, College Wesleyan Church, Marion, Indiana, June 7, 2009. All subsequent quotes from Charlie are from this interview.

[36]It should be noted that Open House is not the only teaching time. Charlie is quick to point people toward the Sunday morning Sunday school class in which he leads the youth group through more traditional biblical exhortation. Charlie's goal is to expose students to God talk as well as the Scripture narrative in order to better understand what God looks and sounds like.

about your life." More people came forward to testify, he explained, when they understood testifying was "simply talking about who they are naturally and who they are when they come to know Jesus Christ and how they've changed." Charlie explains the rationale behind his decision to incorporate testimonies within a weekly service: "If I want teenagers to talk about who they are in Christ in a natural, normal way, I have to give them a safe environment where they can actually talk about it where they won't be mocked or made fun of or embarrassed. They've got to figure it out some place." That place, Charlie hopes, is Open House. "We want them to be able to talk in a regular, consistent way about who they are. And maybe by doing it in here, it will help them do it wherever they are."

Drawing from table 5.3, the testimonies given at Open House are of a more formal nature. Despite the appearance of being loosely constructed, Open House is thoughtfully planned out behind the scenes. There are other spaces in which a teenager can testify as well. In addition to Open House, the youth group's small groups provide an informal space for more spontaneous testimonies to emerge. At Open House, however, there is a precise time and place for a testimony. The testimonies given tend to oscillate between ordered and spontaneous. Those testifying do not simply stand and speak when they are so inclined. Those desiring to testify meet with Charlie ahead of time for an informal discussion concerning the content of their testimonies. "I meet with them ahead of time, but you never know what's going to happen. As much as I try to work with them in advance, it's still risky. But that's why we're here," he says, speaking of the numerous adult leaders present. "So if it does take a weird turn, it's easy to get him back on track and bring it to a close."

Charlie's idea of teenagers testifying does not mean giving them a blank slate to speak. He might not know precisely what they are going to say, but that does not mean the service is spontaneous by any means. "It's pretty calculated," he says. "I'm a big fan of pastoring a service. [It means] being sensitive to what's going on. So I might not be on stage, but I'm watching and sensing and thinking." After all, Charlie says, "they're kids." Charlie is quick to acknowledge the dangers that come with testifying and speaks of the importance of having an intentional, behind-the-scenes director of these events. A competent leader is essential, he explains, because "if you're not a craftsman at knowing how to shape it, you know, it takes wild turns to the right and the left and next thing you know you've been there an hour and a half and you've gotten nothing accomplished."

When I spoke to Paul Hontz about the testimonies taking place in my home church he shared something similar:

> The pastor isn't just an uninvolved, neutral person to try to make transitions between testimonies. The pastor is engaged and must be engaged in shepherding the testimony—I don't mean controlling it, . . . but I think that the pastor has to shepherd the moment and by that I mean the pastor has a responsibility to help the one who is speaking to share.[37]

On more than one occasion Charlie has intervened at Open House to help shape the service. "These are the rarities," Charlie says. He explains how he stands in the back so that the testifier can see him at all times. The speakers know prior to the service to not be surprised if Charlie intervenes. They know "if I sense something then I always have the prerogative to come beside them, and not interrupt them, but to come alongside of them. So we talk about that pre-service."[38] And it is Charlie's carefully thought through intervention and the "safety nets" he has created that have led this church to a *responsible* practice of testimony.

Throughout our interview Charlie stressed the importance of remembering that teenagers are "kids" and should not be expected to have the emotional maturity of a thirty-year-old. What is more, he explains, there is almost an obligation on the youth leader's part to make sure that a teenager is not going to stand up in front of her peers and either make a fool of herself or woefully mislead others. Speaking of the behind-the-scenes planning he does, Charlie explains, "There is never a moment where if [a teenager] were to fail there's not a safety net, which I think lends freedom to them. They know [about the safety nets]; *they feel more comfortable.*" Now we turn to what these safety nets are.

---

[37]Paul Hontz, interview by Amanda Drury, digital recording, Central Wesleyan Church, Holland, Michigan, December 19, 2011.

[38]Alcock interview.

Exercising Discernment in a Responsible Practice of Testifying: Testimonial Troubleshooting

What if the testimony is simply untrue? Of course, the thought of teenagers testifying might send some youth workers into a panic. And for good reason. Allowing teenagers to speak publicly of God is opening the door for them to make a mistake they might not have otherwise made. There is always a chance teenagers can stand up and simply say something false. When a public testimony is given that is untrue the youth pastor has three choices: (1) allow the mistake to slide with the hope that the listeners will be able to discern the truth, (2) correct the mistake in private or (3) correct the mistake in public. The response will largely depend on the circumstances. There is probably very little harm in allowing a false piece of trivia to slide by without correction, for example if the student says San Diego instead of San Francisco or attributes a verse to the apostle Paul instead of the apostle Peter. There is a level of grace that we can expect from listeners when receiving a testimony from what is probably a very anxious speaker. One pastor explained to me that you have to trust the congregation to filter through small, harmless inconsistencies within a testimony.[39]

> Just because something is true does not mean we should testify to its existence. Just because we believe we have witnessed some kind of divine interaction in our lives does not mean we need to testify. We see multiple instances in Scripture where Jesus does something miraculous and then instructs the witnesses to keep quiet about what they have seen.

It is a bit more difficult when the error made needs some kind of correction. Should that correction take place in private or public? Is the speaker solely affected by the error, or is there a chance someone listening could be negatively affected as well?

My home church often gives "interview testimonies" where it is expected that the pastor will jump in from time to time to ask a question or make a point of clarification. Granted, some of these questions might be a bit leading, perhaps something like: "You talk about getting baptized

---

[39]Hontz interview.

in order to make your parents happy, but is there any sense of wanting to do this out of obedience to God?" Often, the pastor explains, the testifier is grateful and perhaps even relieved to have a bit of guidance or a chance for clarification. "Oh yeah," he might say, "that's the big reason why I'm doing this," and then go on to elucidate. When correction was appropriate, this pastor says, "I would gently and carefully address that, and almost always when I would do that the person would say, 'Oh yes, that's what I meant,' and they would be appreciative of that help."[40]

The trick in this kind of correction is to do so in a way that will not embarrass the speaker. The teenagers in Charlie's youth group know that there is a chance he will join them on stage to participate in the testimony. Charlie walking on stage is not a sign of failure; rather, it is a recognized and accepted action that occasionally takes place. Charlie's presence on stage is often during emotionally charged times, and it appears as if the teenagers see his presence as a comfort. One can almost see a sense of relief on the teenagers' faces that someone has come alongside to help carry the burden.

What if the testimony is true but should not be shared publicly? Perhaps even more frightening is the testimony given that is true but should not be shared. Charlie speaks of one of the well-respected youth group members who stood to testify and ended up confessing an addiction to cutting and self-mutilation. Everything he said was true. The problem was, however, that this young man was not only sharing too vulnerably from his own life, he was also giving a very clinical, detailed description of *how* to self-mutilate. "It was pretty cathartic," Charlie said. "It was pretty deep, and [it] was borderline."[41] Charlie was quick to join him on stage, very conscious of the fact that he did not want to embarrass the young man and his heartfelt sharing. Charlie explained that he walked up on stage, sat next to the young man and simply said, "'Evan, I just want to pray with you. I think right now is an appropriate time 'cause there's gotta be people here who are struggling with this right now.' ... And then [after praying] I'll say, 'Evan, why don't you close us out. Do you have something that you want to say?' And he goes on and I'm sitting

---

[40]Ibid.
[41]Alcock interview.

right there next to him."[42] Though it may sound counterintuitive, there seems to be something about public space that on occasion can prompt deeper, at times inappropriate, sharing; in some ways, public space may hold similarities with online space. I remember a seventh grader who would not dream of walking up to a boy and declaring she recently discovered stretch marks on her thighs yet did not have a problem making such a declaration as her Facebook status. The false sense of security that comes with dimmed lights or in staring into a sea of faces may prompt too intimate of sharing. Of course, others might argue that the cover of night is the perfect opportunity to testify because of the safe, intimate feelings it creates. Regardless of where one lands on the lighting issue, carefully established safety nets are entirely necessary in protecting a teenager from him- or herself.

Just because something is true does not mean we should testify to its existence. Just because we believe we have witnessed some kind of divine interaction in our lives does not mean we need to testify. We see multiple instances in Scripture where Jesus does something miraculous and then instructs the witnesses to keep quiet about what they have seen. And so when Jesus raises Jairus's daughter from the dead, he tells the overwhelmed parents to not tell anyone what has happened (Lk 8:56). When Jesus is transfigured before his disciples' eyes he instructs them to not tell anyone what they have seen until he is raised from the dead (Mt 17:9). The many stories of this nature should be highlighted within youth groups to expose teenagers to the idea that there are times when we should refrain from testifying. Of course, knowing when to speak and when to refrain is a difficult task, and we would be wise to equip our teenagers to ask the self-scrutinizing questions "Is this something that should be shared?" and "Is now the right time to share?" Just because God has intersected someone's life does not mean that person should publicly share what has occurred. We can serve as sounding boards for our teenagers on the appropriateness of their testimony.

What if the testimony does not have a point or is not edifying? There are some testimonies that simply do not appear to be edifying. The

---

[42]Name has been changed.

teenager speaks primarily of herself and her own experiences without any acknowledgment of the divine. One former youth pastor recalled a "famous testifier" of the 1970s who toured various churches testifying to his former life as a Satanist. This was certainly a sensational testimony that gripped the attention of those listening. However, this youth pastor explains, almost the entirety of the testimony concerned his life prior to Christ in such a way that his prior life was somewhat glorified. What he shared was sensational, but it was not edifying.[43]

Charlie could not help but laugh when he told me about the teenager whose testimony revolved around how great the former youth pastor was. It was not a big deal, Charlie explains, yet there was little edification taking place. In this particular case, Charlie chose to simply shrug and let it pass. In other cases, the guidelines given earlier for interrupting a false testimony may apply. Some may choose to join the testifier on stage and reframe what has been shared in a more edifying light. So in the case of the above situation, Charlie might have chosen to join the student on stage and end with a time of prayer, thanking God for the ways in which God used the former youth pastor to shape the youth group.

What if the testimony seems to never end? Normally, Charlie explains, the testimonies given at Open House are between seven and ten minutes. On at least one occasion, however, a testimony went long. Charlie speaks of intervening when a particular testimony reached twenty-seven minutes. In this particular case Charlie went forward to pray with the student, though often he only has to make a particular hand signal from the back of the room that had been prearranged with the student as a sign to wrap things up.[44]

What if the student freezes and the testimony never begins or is unexpectedly short? Public speaking can be terrifying. In an effort to spare

---

[43]He goes on to explain: "In the seventies, if you had been a Satanist and were converted, you could actually get on the speaking circuit. At every youth conference they would want you to come. Later there were drugs. There was sort of a reaction. That was the end of the testimony era. . . . Look, you don't have to be a Satanist and get converted to have a testimony. . . . This glorifies the sin. . . . Kids were more fascinated with Satanism than faith. . . . *Wittenberg Door* was the first to speak against [the former Satanist]. [His testimony consisted of] 80 percent Satanism, 20 percent 'I was delivered from all of that.' When testimony was at its highest was when it was about to collapse" (Drury interview).

[44]Alcock interview.

teenagers from unnecessary embarrassment, certain safety nets can be put in place for those who stand to testify and either freeze or are unable to articulate what they originally hoped to share. In this case, the youth pastor can come forward as an interviewer to guide them through their testimony. As an alternative, Charlie explains that he always has some kind of PowerPoint presentation ready to go at moment's notice to attempt a smooth transition into the next order of service.

What if the listeners laugh or are disrespectful of the one testifying? Interestingly enough, none of the youth pastors I interviewed cited this as a problem. In fact, all of them stated that the teenagers tend to listen more intently to their peers as opposed to the youth pastors. As one youth pastor put it, "You can hear a pin drop" when a teenager testifies.[45] One student I interviewed spoke of feeling nervous every time a teenager testified. This anxiety produces almost a holy hush in the room. She reasons, "They are probably nervous so I'm nervous for them."[46] Nevertheless, if this is a potential issue in a youth group, it should be addressed *before* it takes place. The goal is not to respond to ridicule but to circumvent it. Youth group leaders afraid of how their teenagers might respond would be wise to carve out some kind of "holy space" at their meetings where certain ground rules are established. Perhaps they light a particular candle indicating they are entering into a holy time where they take very seriously what is said.

The formative testimonies given at Open House did not begin overnight. Introducing the practice of testimony took a few months. At its inception, Charlie admits teenagers had a difficult time looking at him, much less talking to him about their stories. "They would talk to each other," Charlie explains, "but they would never think about talking up front or any of that kind of stuff."[47] Charlie intentionally gave invitations to speak as well as provided opportunities and avenues to talk. And slowly, teenagers began to respond one by one until what was once the anomaly became the norm. Charlie explains:

---

[45]David Kujawa, interview by Amanda Drury, digital recording, Central Wesleyan Church, Holland, Michigan, December 2, 2008.

[46]Madie, interview by Amanda Drury, digital recording, Holland, Michigan, November 19, 2011.

[47]Alcock interview.

I think there's a culture [of testifying] now. We're developing a culture where that's a part of what we do. And so all of a sudden it's taking on its own life; there is momentum behind it. At first only a couple people volunteered, and then it started to grab momentum; and the more people that did, the more people wanted to. We developed a culture where that's what we do.

Testifying that is integral to a youth group's identity grants permission to teenagers to talk about God. Seventeen-year-old Madie is a member of a youth group in Michigan where seniors in high school are invited to share their experiences with God. Madie describes herself as somewhat shy and claims that at one point she would have been hesitant to speak of God in front of her entire youth group. She describes herself as someone whose faith is very important to her but when pushed could not think of a time when she had talked about her faith publicly. After three years of hearing the testimonies of youth group members a bit older than herself, she now has a kind of lens to see how God has been at work in her own life.

Madie was particularly struck by the *kind* of teenagers she saw testify: "I'm pretty shy, so seeing other people that didn't really stand out in our youth group go up there and talk about their lives was really inspiring to me because I'm kinda in the background too."[48] The testimonial culture Madie experienced in her youth group empowered and encouraged her, opening her eyes to the reality that she, too, might have something to say. Madie was scheduled to testify in her youth group shortly after our interview. When I asked if she knew what she was going to say she confessed she was not entirely sure but was actively on the lookout for places where God might be visibly present in her life. This cultivated culture of testimony in Madie's youth group has given Madie an Advent-like lens where she is looking for the presence of God. The youth group has given Madie the ears to hear as she has spent the past three years hearing testimonies from other teenagers. And as of spring 2011, this youth group will have also provided a place where Madie can testify herself. There is a kind of culture that comes along with testifying, and with work, this is a culture that can be cultivated.

What if a teenager attributes something to God that may not be from God? There is always a chance a teenager could stand up and testify

---

[48]Madie interview.

to God's goodness in allowing her volleyball team to demolish their opponents. And there is always a chance that at least one or two of her opponents is sitting in the audience receiving this testimony. What do we do when something is ascribed to God that may not be of God? How do we help our teenagers live in an Advent-like state without encouraging them to name God as the author of every single move? What of the dangers of seeing God everywhere? The danger of instructing a teenager to look for God could be that the teenager sees God in places where God is not necessarily manifesting himself, thereby perhaps taking the Lord's name in vain. What then?

These questions lead us back to the beginning of the chapter where I discussed Advent-like expectation in combination with circumspect language. The more we allow our teenagers to practice this kind of God talk in low-risk settings that allow for follow-up conversations the better we are able to help shape our teenagers into a respectful, appropriate understanding of where and how God works. And so when the teenager praises God for intervening in her volleyball game we might follow up her exclamation with a few questions: "What makes you think God is at work in this situation?" "How do you think God was present with the losing team?" "What if you had lost? How would you feel about God then?" In other scenarios we might ask, "Does this experience resemble any other kind of experience?" "Does this experience look like anything biblical?" If this testimony is given publicly, then these questions might be asked in a testimony interview format. Of course, if it is too late to do an impromptu interview, it is also possible for the youth leader to offer a subtle counter-testimony—a story of how God taught him or her to see something a bit differently.

This is a tricky topic for youth pastors. There is also the danger of a teenager testifying to something God did not necessarily do and the listeners being subsequently turned off. Thankfully, there is more than one way to testify, and if youth leaders find their teenagers are in a position where they are either not speaking respectfully of God or are struggling with crossing some of the boundaries mentioned above (e.g., speaking too long or speaking truthfully at an improper time), there is always the option of pulling back and establishing greater boundaries in practicing testifying. So instead of spontaneous or quasi-spontaneous testimonies, a youth group might decide to embrace ordered testimonies for a time where teenagers write up their understanding of where they saw God at work and go through this narrative with their youth leader before reading their testimony in public. Others may decide to engage in video testimonies. Here you can get the benefits of testifying while maintaining a certain level of control. Edits can be made, follow-up questions asked, and public speaking fears can be somewhat quieted.

Inarticulacy is a problem for mature Christian faith. The solution to inarticulacy is not simply asking people to talk. What we need is for our teenagers to be nurtured to see the world through a spiritual lens that allows them to live in a state of perpetual Advent, looking for the ways in which God interacts with their stories.

The above scenarios are set in a formal structure. Many of these responses can be adapted for more informal settings. In fact, many may find troubleshooting to be easier in informal settings than in formal settings. In the informal settings you have the immediate opportunity to push back or ask a question.

There are also testimonies that attribute to God what some might see as mere coincidence, or mundane aspects of everyday life. I am reminded of fourteen-year-old Olivia who graciously shared with me a testimony she gave during her church's Sunday morning worship service. In front of her peers as well as the adults of her church, Olivia gave a thoughtful testimony that described her understanding of God's intervention in her life from the time she was four up until her current age.[49] It was fascinating to see how her understanding of God changed and matured over the decade. The stories of her four-year-old self revolved around watching God answer her prayers for "a reasonably priced car," a "baby brother" ("I prayed and prayed that it would be a baby boy, and it was. Later they had another boy. So, not only did my prayers bless me with one baby brother, but I was blessed with two amazing little brothers.") and a job for her uncle. She also testifies to God answering prayers for smaller things like lost keys. The cynics among us might be tempted to write this testimony

---

[49]Olivia, interview by Amanda Drury, written record, Grand Rapids, Michigan, January 21, 2012.

off as a stringing together of mere coincidences. To Olivia, however, this was the reality of God at work in her life, and it shaped her accordingly. Furthermore, the affirmation she received for actively seeking God's presence in everyday life experiences nurtured within her a kind of perpetual Advent.

Somewhere along the way, Olivia's God sightings moved from lost car keys to caring for African children orphaned by AIDS. As a teenager, Olivia heard a sermon calling for Christians to fight the AIDS epidemic raging through Africa. It was through this sermon that Olivia claims God spoke to her.

> While I was looking through those [sermon] notes an idea came to my mind. My idea was that for forty days people could read a chapter of Isaiah a day, and then pray for the orphans in Africa. Then after they were done with this they would set aside a dollar for each day so that at the end of the time they would have saved up forty dollars. . . . Then all of the money would be combined and given to the Africa's Child missions. I wasn't expecting a huge response. I did know that me, my dad and my mom were at least going to do it, so I was hoping to raise about $150. . . . However the turnout was a lot more than I expected it to be. . . . [M]y pastor wanted me to get up in front of our church to give it personally to one of the people who works with Africa's Child (she just happened to be in Michigan when all the money was collected). So on a Sunday I got up in front of the church and my pastor asked me some questions about the program, which I named *40 Days to Save.* Then the lady with Africa's Child came up, and my pastor asked me if I had something to for the lady.
>
> I said, "Yes, I have a check for $500 to go to Africa's Child missions." She cried and everyone else clapped. I was mainly happy to just be able to give this gift. I was really happy with the final amount. . . .
>
> I now will be going to Africa this summer with my grandpa and my dad. We will be going to Malawi and South Africa, and I am only going to be fourteen. I have an amazing opportunity to start working on God's calling for me and I am still young. This trip is going to be difficult to raise money for, but if God wants it to be done, then a way will be provided for me to go. That's the God I've come to know and love. God has done some amazing things throughout my life, and although I still have rough patches and difficult times, I know that through Christ all things are possible.[50]

---

[50]Ibid.

Olivia's story is one of perpetual Advent. No doubt that which she attributed to God as a child was affirmed at home and church.

CONCLUSION

Those seeking to incorporate the practice of public testimony within their youth groups may be pleasantly surprised to learn they are not starting from scratch; in fact, many of the practices they already embody may hold potential for making room for testifying. And while these open doors for testifying may hold some danger, youth pastors like Charlie have shown us that when they are done responsibly and with thoughtful preparation and reflection, speakers and listeners alike reap the spiritual fruit.

I can attest to being blessed myself by the conclusion of Olivia's testimony. After describing her process of raising money for AIDS orphans in Africa, Olivia concludes:

> Answered prayers are possible, no matter how small the request or the person. Salvation is possible, even for rough tempered people like me. Raising money with simple ideas and determination is possible because my God cares. God taking a 14 year old girl out of her comfort zone, her time zone, and out of her own continent is possible. *This is my testimony. This is my story. And it's only just begun.*[51]

To all those adolescents whose stories, like Olivia's, are just beginning, may you know and recognize God's present and steadfast love, which invades and permeates our lives over and over again in ways we can only begin to comprehend.

Inarticulacy is a problem for mature Christian faith. The solution to inarticulacy is not simply asking people to talk. It is not necessarily the implementation of a new educational plan on the importance of testifying (though I imagine that would not hurt). What we need is for our teenagers to be nurtured to see the world through a spiritual lens that allows them to live in a state of perpetual Advent, looking for the ways in which God interacts with their stories. When and if this Advent is realized, we must give space and opportunity for our teenagers to practice this newly acquired language in such a way that they might echo the apostle John with both confidence and humility that "I have seen and I testify . . ." (Jn 1:34).

---

[51]Ibid. Emphasis added.

Bibliography

Allport, Gordon W., and Leo Joseph Postman. *The Psychology of Rumor*. New York: Russell & Russell, 1965.

Ammerman, Nancy Tatom. *Everyday Religion: Observing Modern Religious Lives*. Oxford: Oxford University Press, 2007.

Audi, Robert. *Epistemology: A Contemporary Introduction to the Theory of Knowledge*. London: Routledge, 1998.

Augustine. *The Confessions and Enchiridion*. Edited by Albert C. Outler. Philadelphia: Westminster Press, 1955.

Austin, J. L. *How to Do Things with Words*. Cambridge, MA: Harvard University Press, 1975.

Barth, Karl. *Church Dogmatics* II/1. Edinburgh: T & T Clark, 1957.

———. *Church Dogmatics* IV/3. Edinburgh: T & T Clark, 1962.

———. *The Word of God and the Word of Man*. Translated by Douglas Horton. New York: Harper, 1957.

Bauckham, Richard. *Jesus and the Eyewitnesses: The Gospels as Eyewitness Testimony*. Grand Rapids: Eerdmans, 2006.

Berger, Peter L., and Thomas Luckmann. *The Social Construction of Reality: A Treatise in the Sociology of Knowledge*. Garden City, NY: Doubleday, 1966.

Brown, Delwin, Sheila Greeve Davaney and Kathryn Tanner. *Converging on Culture: Theologians in Dialogue with Cultural Analysis and Criticism*. Oxford: Oxford University Press, 2001.

Brown, Raymond Edward. *The Epistles of John*. Garden City, NY: Doubleday, 1982.

Brueggemann, Walter. *Theology of the Old Testament: Testimony, Dispute, Advocacy*. Minneapolis: Fortress, 2005.

Busch, Eberhard. *Karl Barth and the Pietists: The Young Karl Barth's Critique of Pietism and Its Response*. Translated by Daniel W. Bloesch. Downers Grove,

IL: InterVarsity Press, 2004.

Charmaz, Kathy. *Constructing Grounded Theory: A Practical Guide Through Qualitative Analysis*. London: Sage, 2006.

Chopp, Rebecca. *The Power to Speak: Feminism, Language, God*. Eugene, OR: Wipf & Stock, 1991.

———. "Theology and the Poetics of Testimony." *Criterion* 37 (Winter 1998): 2-12.

Coady, C. A. J. *Testimony: A Philosophical Study*. Oxford: Clarendon, 1992.

Collins Winn, Christian T., ed. *From the Margins: A Celebration of the Theological Work of Donald W. Dayton*. Eugene, OR: Pickwick, 2007.

Dayton, Donald W. *Discovering an Evangelical Heritage*. Peabody, MA: Hendrickson, 1988.

Dean, Kenda Creasy. *Almost Christian: What the Faith of Our Teenagers Is Telling the American Church*. Oxford: Oxford University Press, 2010.

Dieter, Melvin E. *The Holiness Revival of the Nineteenth Century*. Lanham, MD: Scarecrow Press, 1996.

Drury, John L. "Barth and Testimony." In *Karl Barth and the Future of Evangelical Theology*. Edited by Christian T. Collins Winn and John L. Drury. Eugene, OR: Pickwick, 2014.

Dykstra, Craig. "Reconceiving Practice in Theological Inquiry and Education." In *Virtues and Practices in the Christian Tradition: Christian Ethics After MacIntyre*, edited by Nancey C. Murphy, Brad J. Kallenberg and Mark Nation, pp. 161-84. Harrisburg, PA: Trinity Press International, 1997.

Florence, Anna Carter. *Preaching as Testimony*. Louisville, KY: Westminster John Knox Press, 2007.

Fowler, Glenn. "Robert Buckhout, Writer and Professor of Psychology, 55." *The New York Times*, December 12, 1990. Accessed September 6, 2011. www .nytimes.com/1990/12/12/obituaries/robert-buckhout-writer-and-professor -of-psychology-55.html.

Guder, Darrell L. *The Continuing Conversion of the Church*. Grand Rapids: Eerdmans, 2000.

Heath, Elaine A. *Naked Faith: The Mystical Theology of Phoebe Palmer*. Eugene, OR: Pickwick, 2009.

Hünermann, Peter, Helmut Hoping, Robert L. Fastiggi, Anne E. Nash and Heinrich Denzinger. *Enchiridion Symbolorum: Compendium of Creeds, Definitions, and Declarations on Matters of Faith and Morals*. San Francisco: Ignatius Press, 2012.

Janes, Reverend Bishop. Introduction to *Pioneer Experiences*, by Phoebe Palmer.

New York: Garland, 1984.

Jenson, Robert W. *Story and Promise: A Brief Theology of the Gospel About Jesus.* Philadelphia: Fortress, 1973.

Jones, Gregory L. "Narrative Theology." In *The Blackwell Encyclopedia of Modern Christian Thought,* edited by Alister E. McGrath, pp. 395-98. Oxford: Blackwell, 1999.

Kegan, Robert. *In Over Our Heads: The Mental Demands of Modern Life.* Cambridge, MA: Harvard University Press, 1994.

Lamarque, Peter. "On Not Expecting Too Much from Narrative." *Mind & Language* 19 (2004): 393-407.

Landauer, Thomas K. *Handbook of Latent Semantic Analysis.* Mahwah, NJ: Lawrence Erlbaum Associates, 2007.

Landauer, Thomas K., and Susan T. Dumais. "A Solution to Plato's Problem: The Latent Semantic Analysis Theory of Acquisition, Induction, and Representation of Knowledge." *Psychological Review* 104, no. 2 (1997): 211-40.

Locke, John. *An Essay Concerning Human Understanding.* New York: Dover Publications, 1959.

Lohr, David. "Meet Benjaman Kyle: The Man with No Identity." AOL News, September 13, 2010. Accessed July 16, 2011. www.aolnews.com/2010/09/13/ meet-benjaman-kyle-the-man-with-no-identity.

Long, Thomas G. *Testimony: Talking Ourselves into Being Christian.* San Francisco: Jossey-Bass, 2004.

MacIntyre, Alasdair C. *After Virtue: A Study in Moral Theory.* Notre Dame, IN: University of Notre Dame Press, 1984.

McAdams, Daniel P. *The Stories We Live By: Personal Myths and the Making of the Self.* New York: W. Morrow, 1993.

McClintock Fulkerson, Mary. *Changing the Subject: Women's Discourses and Feminist Theology.* Eugene, OR: Wipf & Stock, 2001.

McHugh, Adam S. *Introverts in the Church: Finding Our Place in an Extroverted Culture.* Downers Grove, IL: InterVarsity Press, 2009.

Metz, Johann Baptist. "A Short Apology of Narrative." In *Why Narrative?* Edited by Stanley Hauerwas and L. Gregory Jones, pp. 251-62. Grand Rapids: Eerdmans, 1989.

Mezirow, Jack. *Transformative Dimensions of Adult Learning.* San Francisco: Jossey-Bass, 1991.

Niebuhr, H. Richard. *The Meaning of Revelation.* Louisville, KY: Westminster John Knox Press, 2006.

———. "The Story of Our Lives." In *Why Narrative?*, edited by Stanley Hauerwas and L. Gregory Jones, pp. 21-44. Grand Rapids: Eerdmans, 1989.

Osmer, Richard Robert. *Practical Theology: An Introduction*. Grand Rapids: Eerdmans, 2008.

Palmer, Phoebe. *Full Salvation: Its Doctrine and Duties*. Salem, OH: Schmul, 1979.

———. *Promise of the Father*. New York: Garland, 1985.

———. *The Way of Holiness with Notes by the Way: Being a Narrative of Religious Experience Resulting from a Determination to Be a Bible Christian*. New York: Palmer & Hughes, 1981.

Rahner, Karl. *A Rahner Reader*. Edited by Gerald A. McCool. New York: Seabury, 1975.

Ricoeur, Paul. *Essays on Biblical Interpretation*. Edited by Lewis Seymour Mudge. Philadelphia: Fortress, 1980.

———. *Time and Narrative, Volume 1*. Translated by Kathleen McLaughlin and David Pellauer. Chicago: University of Chicago Press, 1984.

Rogers, Frank, Jr. *Finding God in the Graffiti: Empowering Teenagers Through Stories*. Cleveland: Pilgrim Press, 2011.

Root, Jerry. *Space to Speke: The Confessional Subject in Medieval Literature*. New York: Peter Lang, 1997.

Rudd, Anthony. "In Defense of Narrative." *European Journal of Philosophy* 17, no. 1 (2007): 60-75.

Sacks, Oliver W. *An Anthropologist on Mars: Seven Paradoxical Tales*. New York: Knopf, 1995.

———. *The Man Who Mistook His Wife for a Hat and Other Clinical Tales*. New York: Summit Books, 1985.

Sarbin, Theodore R. *Narrative Psychology: The Storied Nature of Human Conduct*. New York: Praeger, 1986.

Smith, Christian. "Is Moralistic Therapeutic Deism the New Religion of American Youth? Implications for the Challenge of Religious Socialization and Reproduction." In *Passing on the Faith: Transforming Traditions for the Next Generation of Jews, Christians and Muslims*, edited by James Heft, pp. 55-74. New York: Fordham University Press, 2006.

———. *What Is a Person? Rethinking Humanity, Social Life, and the Moral Good from the Person Up*. Chicago: University of Chicago Press, 2010.

Smith, Christian, and Melinda Lundquist Denton. *Soul Searching: The Religious and Spiritual Lives of American Teenagers*. Oxford: Oxford University Press,

2005.

Smith, Christian, and Michael Emerson. *American Evangelicalism: Embattled and Thriving*. Chicago: University of Chicago Press, 1998.

Smith, James K. A. *Desiring the Kingdom: Worship, Worldview, and Cultural Formation*. Grand Rapids: Baker Academic, 2009.

Stark, Rodney. *The Rise of Christianity: A Sociologist Reconsiders History*. Princeton, NJ: Princeton University Press, 1996.

Stout, Jeffrey. *Ethics After Babel: The Languages of Morals and Their Discontents*. Boston: Beacon Hill, 1988.

———. "Liberal Society and the Language of Morals." *Soundings* 69 (1986): 32-59.

Taylor, Charles. *The Ethics of Authenticity*. Cambridge, MA: Harvard University Press, 1992.

Tertulian. *Apology*. Translated by T. R. Glover. Cambridge, MA: Harvard University Press, 1984.

Wesley, John. *The Journal of John Wesley*. Edited by Hugh Price Hughes and Percy Livingstone Parker. Grand Rapids: Christian Classics Ethereal Library, 2000. www.ccel.org/ccel/wesley/journal.pdf.

———. "The Witness of the Spirit." In *The Works of John Wesley, Volume V*, pp. 111-23. Grand Rapids: Baker, 1978.

Wheatley, Richard. *The Life and Letters of Mrs. Phoebe Palmer*. New York: Garland, 1984.

White, Charles Edward. *The Beauty of Holiness: Phoebe Palmer as Theologian, Revivalist, Feminist, and Humanitarian*. Grand Rapids: Francis Asbury Press, 1986.

Name and Subject Index

Scripture Index

Finding the Textbook You Need

The IVP Academic Textbook Selector
is an online tool for instantly finding the IVP books
suitable for over 250 courses across 24 disciplines.

---

ivpacademic.com
